STORIES TO TELL ...

Of Lives Lived Well

Enid Cleaves

"STORIES TO TELL of Lives Lived Well," by Enid Cleaves. ISBN 978-1-63868-201-1.

Published 2025 by Virtualbookworm.com Publishing Inc., P.O. Box 9949, College Station, TX 77842, US. ©2025, Enid Cleaves. All rights reserved. No part of this publication may be reproduced, stored in a retrieval system, or transmitted in any form or by any means, electronic, mechanical, recording or otherwise, without the prior written permission of Enid Cleaves.

TABLE OF CONTENTS

PROCLIVITY TO LONGEVITY

Dan Buettner, world-renowned longevity expert, explorer and author, has identified several Blue Zones in the world. These are communities, Buettner claims, "where people not only live longer, but also enjoy a high quality of life in their old age."

Eight communities in southwest Florida have achieved Blue Zones Community certification for developing healthy standards of living recommendations (including diet and lifestyle) for their residents. Dodge County in Wisconsin was added to list in 2020. But, could there be more?

Areas in north/central Wisconsin might qualify for Blue Zone communities: blue lakes and rivers, blue skies...plenty of opportunities for participating in outdoor sports and exercise, growing gardens with healthy foods, and developing a positive attitude—simply by looking out one's window at the beauty of nature.

Since I became a widow several years ago and sought to find new friends and activities, I met several "older women" still active with much to offer to the world. Opposed to "feeling blue," these women had a great outlook on life. Instead of dwelling on the trials and tribulations life might bring, they maintained a state of mind of fulfillment and consolation. The stories in this book are about a few of these women: their accomplishments, experiences, and attitudes. Jules Renard, well-known French novelist and playwright believes "It is not how old you are, but how you are old."

Charles M. Schulz, a well-known cartoonist and creator of Charlie Brown and Snoopy, once said "Just remember, once you're over the hill, you begin to pick up speed!" As opposed to "going downhill fast," I take this to mean speed in accomplishing and achieving one's goals and objectives!

There is a song "Blue Eyes Crying in the Rain" written by Fred Rose. I've especially enjoyed listening to Willie Nelson sing it (in person once)! There are different meanings attributed to this song, but the first verse seems to indicate a man looking back on a broken relationship.

In the twilight glow I see them
Blue eyes crying in the rain
When we kissed goodbye and parted
I knew we'd never meet again
Love is like a dying ember
And only memories remain
And through the ages I'll remember
Blue eyes crying in the rain
Some day when we meet up yonder
We'll stroll, hand in hand again
In a land that knows no parting
Blue eyes crying in the rain

There's another version of this song, penned by a poet/songwriter who lived in northern Wisconsin; namely, my late husband. It's about senior citizens driving up the interstate highway from the big cities to their peaceful getaway in the "Northwoods." Sometimes on a Friday afternoon we would find ourselves in a mini traffic jam. The verse goes something like this:

> In the twilight glow I see them,
> Up from Janesville and Des Plaines.
> Through the ages I'll remember
> Blue hairs driving in my lane.

Well, I guess you have to be a certain age to know that the term "blue hairs" referred to older people who dyed their gray hair a darker color. Some hair dyes would turn their hair into a shade of blue or purple.

Persons from a younger generation sometimes complain that senior citizens drive slowly in the outer lane, thus clogging up that "fast" lane! My mom, bless her soul, occasionally was a "blue hair." I once took her on vacation to southern California. We walked across the bridge into Mexico one afternoon. While window shopping, a youngster of probably twelve or thirteen approached us on the sidewalk. He suddenly stopped walking, looked at my mom and uttered in his best English, "Lady, why you got purple hair?" It wasn't long after that when Mom let her hair go back to her natural gray!

A friend, in her mid-80s, dyed her hair purple. (She also drives a bright blue Ford Mustang convertible!) Another friend, in the same age group, just got a speeding ticket. One had plastic surgery done here and there on her body parts. Another wrote two books while in her mid-90s. Two local women escaped to freedom during the Czech resistance, a harrowing all-night trek, crossing the Danube River, into Austria. The oldest woman featured in this book, is now 103. Of Norwegian heritage, she makes enough lefse every Christmas season to feed a small country! The women you will read about in the following chapters were born in, lived in, or have strong ties to north/central Wisconsin. Each has a story to tell about her life's experiences.

**HATS OFF TO THESE WOMEN--
WHATEVER THEIR HAIR COLOR!**

FROM PRAGUE TO PARADISE

Vlasta Polacek was born in December 1924, daughter of a Hungarian/Austrian Countess. From her home northern Hungary, surrounded by the beautiful Carpathian Mountains, it would be a long and arduous journey to Manitowish Waters, Wisconsin where Vlasta and daughter Val Bogdan would call their home.

Vlasta, Countess Egli's daughter, would also hold the title of "Countess" as would every girl born of a woman holding that title. Vlasta's dad reminded her to be humble, saying "You can't eat from that."

In 1926 the family moved from Hungary to Prague, Czechoslovakia (formerly Bohemia and now the Czech Republic or Czechia as it is sometimes called) to "upgrade their life." Later, Vlasta recalled, her dad wore a uniform and probably was either in civil service or the military. He was involved in politics as well.

Vlasta remembered her mother to be "an extremely beautiful person" who was "open, easy to talk with and very helpful." Talented and driven, Vlasta already had a love for art in the fourth grade. The art teacher wouldn't exhibit her drawings with those of other students and "discouraged her budding talent." A bit rebellious and with poor eyesight, Vlasta was unhappy with the relationship she held with her instructor. "My mom helped me to get out of the class by persuading a doctor to write an excuse."

At age nine, Vlasta was accepted into the renowned Children's Choir, heard on the radio throughout the country. Her sister Franceska, thirteen months older, was a soloist in the choir. She went on to become an opera singer.

By mid March 1939 Czechoslovakia was under Nazi occupation. (The Germans would occupy Prague until 1945.)

Adolph Hitler spent a night in the Prague Castle, proudly proclaiming his new possession. The Castle became headquarters of Nazi Reinhard Heydrich, Reich Protector of Bohemia. According to rumor, anyone who placed the Bohemian crown on his head would die within a year. Heydrich did so and was killed by Czech resistance fighters while on his way to the castle. His son died within a year later, victim of a traffic accident

Prague castle, 7,500 sq. feet, is the largest castle complex in the world.

During that period 18-year-old Vlasta was sent to work in a factory that made ammunition. Here, when she found time, she made little figurines out of scrap metal. Meanwhile, she obtained some business training. Recognizing this, the "Big Boss" singled her out to be his secretary. Vlasta had more spare time in this position. So, when the boss was gone, she would paint porcelain vases and sell them to people who came into the office!

In 1941 the factory was bombed; workers were herded into shelters that had little heat. When they emerged, they saw the factory was in ruins. Vlasta walked home to find a bomb near her house that had not been detonated. Turned away, she walked to a convent where she was reunited with her family. Here they stayed four days until all was safe.

German soldiers were everywhere. Men standing by the statue in Wenceslas Square were all crying. At home her father was crying. Every time Vlasta heard sirens, she cried too.

Prisoners defused the bombs; in return, they gained their freedom. Tears came to Vlasta's eyes as she recalled those frightful days. The war was still so vivid in her memory.

In 1945 Vlasta became a live speaker for news programs on Radio Free Europe, set up by the United States Central Intelligence Agency to deliver news to countries that had important relationships with the U.S.

Fighting broke out in Wenceslas Square.
The monument of the good king Wenceslas,
later named a saint, still stands.

The Prague Uprising began on May 5, 1945, attempting to liberate the city of Prague from German occupation. Hitler had already killed himself in his underground bunker.

The Russian Liberation Army, who had fought for the Germans, now supported the Czechs. U. S. General George S. Patton's Third Army joined forces. Allied Commander Dwight D. Eisenhower kept the warring factions out of Prague. Czech resistance leaders came out of hiding to join the fight, and Czech citizens left their homes.

Vlasta was one of the revolutionists. She didn't tell her mother where she was going. She was gone five days and five nights, helping to build barricades against German tanks and doing what she could to aid the uprising. Her father was already fighting—somewhere. Men who didn't have guns used pitchforks and knives.

Vlasta filled the large pockets of her dress with ammunition given to her by civilians to transport to those who did have guns. Czech women and children were being used as shields. Revolutionists built barricades and turned over streetcars for protection. A man standing next to Vlasta was shot. He gave his gun to Vlasta. She fired back. "I think I shot someone," she offered, "but I don't know."

In March 1948 Prime Minister Edvard Beneš, son of the first Czechoslovakian president, was found dead under a 45-foot-high window. It was reported that he jumped from the window, committing suicide. Others believed differently: He didn't agree with the communists so the Germans had thrown him out the window.

The revolution lasted only a few days, but was followed by two decades of occupation by Russian communists.

It was time for Vlasta to return home, but the walk was not safe. She made her way via roof tops.

Life under the communist control grew worse. Citizens had no privacy and homes were subject to search. People could no longer enjoy free speech and were imprisoned readily for minor actions such as signing petitions or complaints. The wealthy were given less extravagant homes than they were accustomed to and forced to do menial jobs.

A precarious atmosphere, dangerous and unstable, existed in the weeks and months to follow. Purges of military leaders, politicians, Catholics and Jewish residents began in the 1950s. Nearly 200 were executed without a fair trial.

An underground society existed. Contingent plans were made as things got worse. The Polaceks were planning how they could leave their home to escape to a safer environment. By this time their own male family members had been imprisoned. The harsh life and inhumane treatment eventually led to their death.

It was early December 1950. The time was right. A knock came on family's door. An atypical greeting was given; it was the code. The visitors were invited in. They quickly explained that the next morning the family must dress in their usual clothes, taking with them only the following items: money, jewelry, brandy and a towel.

That night Countess Egli and her daughters, Vlasta and Franceska, burned their pictures and important papers and packed baskets full of their good clothes with instructions to the lady who tended to stoves and furnaces in the building to give them to the "society lady" for distribution.

Morning came; the family left their nice three-bedroom apartment forever. Countess Egli, Vlasta with her own three-year-old daughter, Val, and Franceska with her young son, Karl, walked to a nearby park that they frequently visited. Vlasta wore her new red coat, nylon stockings, and comfortable walking shoes. After a short time, they would mosey over to the nearby train station and purchase tickets to a destination about 30 minutes away. Here they would be met by two men from the "underground movement." To this day Val remembers the smell of their leather coats that made "crinkly" noises when they walked.

There was a car waiting for them, but it was broken down and needed repair. They couldn't wait. A taxi was hailed, although it was dangerous because one did not know whether to trust the driver. One of the two underground men sat in front. They picked up two other men along the way. Soon the taxi driver came to a stop and ordered, "Everyone out; I have family, and I know what you are doing. I am not going further." The man in front pulled a gun on the driver and stayed with him while the others got out of the car and started walking. What was to have been a two-hour walk turned out to be a nightmare lasting 11-1/2 hours!

It was snowing; the moon was out. The group, including the male guides, trudged through a forest, finally coming to a field where pheasants were kept. The birds would become noisy if they were disturbed. Guards were spotted in towers surrounding the open fields. "We have to hide now," one of the men said. So, they hid in a haystack for a short time. Vlasta described her vision. "A hand in the wind moved the clouds over the moon; it was a miracle." Darkness was on their side.

The adults crouched low to the ground, not to scare the pheasants, and started walking again. Val remembers stopping at times to remove the water from her shoes. Her navy-blue coat was not keeping her warm. Her slightly-older cousin was a "noisy, whining kid." They had to tranquilize him and carry him a lot. Val, though nodding off frequently, walked most of the way herself. "I don't remember being scared," she reminisced, but more like she was "just holding my mother's hand, on some kind of adventure."

The group approached a bridge over a wild river. Again, they saw men with rifles. They quietly broke the ice at the edge and waded waist deep into the strong current. One of the underground men carried Countess Egli. Vlasta and Franceska carried the children. On the other side they stopped. Vlasta recalled that the men "rubbed our cold legs with brandy" after first giving her a sip! Their towels were used to further dry themselves; nevertheless, their coats were soaking wet like freezing ice. From here it was "field on field on field...hours and hours of walking." Apathy set in.

At daybreak they came to a valley. Here they were told to rest. They fought sleep, knowing that hypothermia could set in. They must keep awake! The men left. Would they return, or were the family left here to die?

Vlasta realized it was December 12th—her 27th birthday! In a semi-conscious state of mind Vlasta had another vision. "I saw my grammar school with yellow geraniums in the window. It was coming close, then disappeared. In reality Vlasta's brother-in-law, Karl, was walking toward them. He had been told by the underground men to come to Vienna. There were hugs and tears...but two more hours to walk. The group's "preservation instinct" had persevered for 9-1/2 hours; they knew that they could make it the rest of the way!

14

Cars were waiting for them in Vienna. "People from one car came out and rubbed us," Vlasta remembers. They offered glögg wine, hot chocolate for the children, and woolen socks. Then they were driven to the Windsor Hotel where "people in the hotel were applauding" them for their perseverance during their arduous trip to Austria.

Vlasta saw her reflection in the mirror. "We looked terrible. I could scarcely recognize myself." The group was offered hot baths and comfortable beds with feather comforters. They slept for 36 hours. Upon wakening they were given medical attention and a hot meal: wiener schnitzel (a thin breaded veal cutlet) and potato salad (still Val's favorite today)!

The rest of the story is anticlimactic, but meaningful. Franceska won a contest in Vienna that landed her the lead role in *Madame Butterfly*. A cab was sent for her, the whole family piled in and made the move to Germany. Both Franceska and Vlaska were employed by Radio Free Europe (RFE) in Munich.

In 1956 the family received visas and were sent by RFE to New York City. A friend told them about a large Czech community in Chicago. Ten days later they took a train to Chicago!

Vlasta was hired to design towels for Windsor Textiles. Co-workers soon taught her four very important English words: "I want a raise."

Before long Vlasta learned that a company down the street needed someone to plan and design display windows. Did she have the proper experience? "I lied; I had never done windows but told them that I had." She got the job at Montgomery Ward and was soon painting murals on their walls. The murals served as a background for clothing she selected from the catalog, pinned on to the mannequins she made out of chicken-wire forms. The job became too much. Besides, she wasn't getting credit for her work or paid a fair wage.

Vlasta enrolled in a fine arts education class at Triton College in River Grove, Illinois (just southeast of O'Hare International Airport). While living in Chicago, Vlasta met Charlie who would become her second husband. He loved to fish, and the couple vacationed frequently near Ladysmith, Wisconsin.

In the early 1980s daughter Val met Kenny Bogdan who brought her up to Lake Nokomis near Tomahawk, Wisconsin. Kenny had been coming to the area with his family since he was six months old. Soon married, the couple began to look for a resort to purchase and discovered the area where they would settle.

Before Charlie passed away in February 1989, Val and Kenny would send him videos of the Manitowish Waters area, about 40 miles from Michigan's Upper Peninsula.

After Charlie's death, Vlasta felt that "she could no longer be in the house" that the two had shared. There were just too many memories. "Take me to where you two always vacation," she asked her daughter. That summer the couple brought Vlasta "up north."

The area reminded her of the region near their family cottage close to Prague—the forest trails she hiked, the river she swam, the streams she rock-hopped to cross. A flood of wonderful memories danced through her head. She purchased a home in Manitowish Waters on Spider Lake, with 18 acres of towering pines, birch trees and hardwoods in the center of the beautiful ten-lake Manitowish chain of lakes. Coincidently, but quite appropriately, the property was located on "Memory Lane."

Vlasta always knew that she would be happy here. From a window she watched a group of ravens, with a white bird in the center. A morning fog lifted; only the white bird remained. The dove followed her around the yard and cooed outside her window. She named it "Charlie" after her late husband. She believed it was a sign that her husband approved of her move. From that point on she "was never alone."

17

In April 1995 Val went to a "starving artist garage sale." She met a lady there, and two weeks later got a phone call from her. Did she want to rent space in a local building and open a gallery? Val's first reaction was that "it was too crazy an idea." The rent would be cheap though, and it was for the summer only.

Vlasta and Val opened the doors to their gallery on Mother's Day that year. In October 1997 the local hardware store decided to turn the building into condominiums. Vlasta purchased the one next to the post office, and the ladies moved their art from across the street into their new gallery! The Artists Palette became a cooperative gallery for local artists to display and sell their art creations.

Vlasta "primarily painted still-life portraits prior to moving to Wisconsin." Here, she "started painting wild life for the first time," mostly from her own photographs. Many of these are now in private collections throughout Wisconsin and Illinois. She always loved to do etchings and received many awards for her work. A museum in Lidice in the Czech Republic sought her out as their first representative from the United States.

Val specialized in custom-made stained and fused glass designs and dichroic jewelry items. Dichroic glass "with its various metal powders coating it, transmits a rainbow of phenomenal colors."

Northern Wisconsin brought back the secure feeling of home and gave Vlasta and her family "the sense of belonging to this naturally beautiful part of our country." Strife and dissension had given way to peace and happiness.

Vlasta passed away at age 93 on July 1, 2019 at her home on Memory Lane. She is remembered for her spirit, patriotism, courage, dedication, love of family and, of course her artistic talents.

Vlasta holds a picture of the white dove she named Charlie. Behind her is a youthful self-portrait.

URBAN LEGEND

Edye Urban lifts her acoustic guitar off the rack on the wall in her senior-living apartment in Neenah, Wisconsin. At our request, she belts out one of her favorite songs, "Crazy," an early 1960s country tune written by Willie Nelson and made popular by Patsy Cline. One song leads to another. She opens her apartment door to the hallway; soon other residents hear the music and enter to join in the impromptu songfest. Another musician hurries down the hall to his apartment to fetch his guitar.

Edye was born on May 1, 1932 in Lenoir, North Carolina, a small city in the beautiful Brushy Mountain range, a spur of the larger Blue Ridge Mountains. Her dad was a choir director at the local Baptist church. Edye was a natural, singing in church and on local radio before she had even entered grade school.

By the time she was in second grade, Edye's parents had divorced. She remained in the family home with her father and two siblings. Neither her brother nor her sister was interested in music, but Edye and her father would come home from church on Sunday mornings only to continue singing gospel songs from the swing on

21

their large porch. When there was a church music convention in another town, Edye's dad would drive in his two-seated truck with Edye and as many parishioners as would fit in the back of the pickup truck!

During summers Edye spent time with her mother in Ohio. One day, a traveling salesman stopped in and sold her mom an insurance policy. "Urbie" found reason to stop in regularly and pursued Edye for the next two years. In 1950, now 18, Edye married Urban Urban!

The couple move to a "non-urban" setting in southern Door County, near Casco, Wisconsin. They bought a farmhouse outside of town--the very house that Urbie was born in. It had been in the family for 150 years. Here they raised three children: Greg, Robin and Roxanne.

Edye kept up her singing, even bought a couple of how-to books and learned to play the guitar. Soon she and two other gal friends formed a group called the "Pepper Shakers." With very little experience, they nevertheless got noticed and were invited to perform at a local fund-raising event. "I only knew four songs," Edye lamented, but we played them over and over in different order! Their audience loved them.

Edye made costumes for herself and the other two musicians. They wore their "short sparkly skirts," and high boots as they performed around the area. Jo played the drums; Lois, base guitar. Edye reminisces, "We didn't sound too good...but we looked good!" They were getting noticed.

White boots are made for tappin'....

Larry Miller noticed Edye at a local club. He had his own musical group but now wanted to become a manager. It was a new phase. The Edye Lenore Show (Edye and three male performers) was formed, and she was on her way!

Nashville: Here we come!

Edye's group recorded several songs in Nashville under the K-Ark and later Jem labels, including a couple of her own compositions. At Tootsies Orchid Lounge, a local club and hangout for musicians, she met and become friends with stars such as Willie Nelson, Roy Clark, Billy "Crash" Craddock, Little Jimmy Dickens and Buck Owens.

She joined Owens for a show in Nashville, toured a bit with O.B. McClinton, and appeared on the Hee-Haw stage several times as the featured female singer. Larry Miller was now producer and Master of Ceremonies of the Hee Haw Revue—an American television variety show featuring country music and humor with the fictional rural "Kornfield Kounty" as the backdrop.

Edye performed three separate times at Country Music Showcase during Fun Fare, a week-long event attended by some 15,000 country music fans. It was "a dream come true!"

Wealthy Nashville estate owners would throw magnificent parties for the musicians who performed at the concerts, usually in large tents erected on their properties. At one such party "Little Jimmy" Dickens offered Edye a spot in his tour group. She refused, "I've got a husband and a family" and felt it would take her away from them for too long.

From this exposure, however, Edye did sign on to shorter, week-long tours throughout the Midwest with the Harry King Cole show ("Weeping Willie" of Hee-Haw fame). In 1975 she toured the northeast states including New York, Ohio, Pennsylvania and Indiana.

Sometimes Edye's daughter, Roxanne, would accompany her on tour, but it was a balancing act for the entertainer with frequent traveling and being able to spend time with her family at home. So, she left the big city and bright lights to return to the family farm in Casco. Here Edye would join up with a popular Wisconsin country group, Walt Hess and the Rim Shots, appearing at nearby pubs, family events, and even barn dances! One year, while she was on vacation, Edye delighted crowds at various pubs in Ireland!

Edye continued to play in local clubs near Casco. Her play list had grown over the years to about 400 songs!

Eventually, Urbie developed cancer. For the next ten years Edye devoted her time to being his caregiver. Urbie passed away in 2009.

In time, Edye moved from the farmhouse into a senior living apartment in Neenah, Wisconsin, closer to Roxanne. Edye would still play her guitar almost every day, alone in her living room.

On Wednesdays she would join resident musicians who played in the commons area.

Occasionally Walt (from the Rim Shots) and musicians from Door County would drive down to Neenah to visit, reminisce about old times and play a little music.

Music has always been "a very big part of my life" Edye went on to say. "There were so many nice people to work with. I made a lot of friends; most of them are gone."

When she turned 88, Edye claimed it was getting hard for her to recall so much of the past. Yet she claimed to remember the words of at least 250 songs and would belt one out upon request!

It's Crazy what life offers, what you take and what you leave. But for Edye *Crazy* is enthusiastic. *Crazy* is passionate. *Crazy* is fervent. *Crazy* is defined as all of the above-- in both of Edye's favorite worlds: family and music.

Edye entertains a few friends at daughter
Roxanne's home in Oshkosh, Wisconsin.

Edye passed away on November 24, 2023 at the senior living home in Appleton, Wisconsin, where she had lived for several months. She was 91 years of age. The day before, Thanksgiving Day, she had enjoyed dinner with her family.

A funeral was held at the Catholic Church in Casco, Wisconsin. Afterwards friends and relatives congregated at Red's Pub and Grill in Algoma.

Overlooking Lake Michigan, it was a favorite place where Edye once performed.

To quote from Edy's obituary:

> Edye embodied a joyful and graceful spirit. She was a "quiet yet influential trailblazer, a beacon of kindness and goodness. Her absence leaves an unfillable void, but her memory and legacy continue to inspire and warm the hearts of those she touched.

OCTO WOMAN

Berniece Krogwold knows how to make *perfect* lefse (a Norwegian flat bread); she's been doing it for 87 years!

Berniece celebrated her 102nd birthday on Valentine's Day 2024. Friends and family from North Dakota, Minnesota, Colorado, Texas, Ohio, and throughout Wisconsin congregated at her home in Amherst Junction, WI to celebrate her life. By the way, her surviving sisters include Doris (age 99), Ruth (96) and Mary Lou (93)! Also, when Berniece talks about "back in the nineties," she means *her* nineties—not the calendar nineties!

A couple of interesting notes: Another Amherst native, Herbert Wolding, reached age 111 on the 15th of October, 2023. He was the oldest living person in the United States. Wolding passed away, however, on November 17 of that year. Ruth Stryzewski takes the (birthday) cake! She turned 112 on February 20, 2024, to make her the oldest living resident in Wisconsin! Sadly, Ruth passed away in November of that year. The oldest person to ever live in the United States was Sarah Knauss. She died on December 30, 1999 at the age of 119 years and 97 days.

Back to Berniece! She shared homemade lefse with those gathered for her birthday from the several pounds still left in her large freezer. She usually runs out of the delicacy in November, when it's time to stock up for another Christmas season!

Berniece grew up on a small hobby farm (one cow, several chickens, three cats and a dog) near Fargo, North Dakota along with five sisters and two brothers. Her mother was an immigrant from Norway; her father was from Washington State. Both parents spoke Norwegian at home. Berniece understands the language, but says she "only speaks a few words." The family made lefse on their wood-burning stove, popular in an era before gas and electricity.

Berniece attended a small rural grade school. When she reached eighth grade, ninth grade was added. In subsequent years three more years of education became available. Berniece was able to graduate with a high school diploma attained in that one-room school!

After high school, she worked in a hospital laundry. There she met a doctor, and later was employed as a nanny for his family as he served the National Guard in various U.S. locations.

Along the way Berniece (Dahl) met, and fell in love with Kenneth Krogwold, friend of the doctor.

They were married in Louisiana, but eventually moved to a farm in his hometown (Amherst, Wisconsin). Here they raised dairy cattle, hogs and beef cattle. The family grew with the birth of their five children: daughter Janet and four boys.

Every November, Berniece spends several days at Janet's home in Boulder Junction, WI for a lefse-making (and Norwegian cookies like krumkake and sandbakkels) event!

When I stopped by, they were in their third day of the mom/daughter lefse marathon (in addition to baking over 300 of the above-mentioned cookies)! I asked if they would share their lefse recipe. Janet wrote down the following:

5 lbs. potatoes, cooked and riced
3 Tbs. melted butter
3 cups flour
Salt

This makes about 20 "rounds" of lefse.

"Where are the directions?" I asked. Janet's response was "You almost have to grow up learning from your relatives who have passed down their knowledge over the years." She warned that "besides just following a recipe, one would need to know more about the process, the utensils, and how to develop the skills needed in rolling, transferring to the lefse griddle, baking and removing at exactly the right time."

"First, you need to use a dry potato such as Green Giant (or russet). We boil the potatoes the night before...and rice them. Then we refrigerate, and in the morning mix it up. Some use a little cream...and if you use too much flour, the dough gets tough." The mixture is formed into rolls and cut into "rounds."

Janet went on to describe their special grooved rolling pin, covered with a lefse sock so the dough doesn't get stuck in the grooves, and a turning stick made from cane tacked onto plywood to flip the lefse sheets on the griddle.

I watched the two-person assembly line work with a perfection only developed with years of experience. I began to understand what Janet meant!

Wisconsin boasts several Norwegian communities. Most have "suppers," often held at Norwegian churches, but sometimes at venues with craft shows, entertainment, or even coinciding with local ski-jumping tournaments (a very popular event in Norway—and in many Wisconsin communities inhabited by Norwegians). The menu usually includes lutefisk (lut fisk, or "lye fish" in Norwegian), Norwegian meatballs, lefse and pastries (along with other sides).

34

Berniece flips the lefse to cook the other side

Generations ago, refrigeration was not available. The fish were dried and then soaked in ashes and water. This in turn produced lye, a preservative. Obviously, the fish had to be rinsed well before eating.

After visiting Norway in 1994, Janet observed, "They don't eat much lutefisk there anymore, but ship it out!" Looking back to her younger days on the farm, she remembers, "We always had lutefisk at Christmas at home...and occasionally at other times. And, if you had lutefisk, you had to have lefse!"

Janet and Berniece invited me to stay for lutefisk and lefse that evening. I declined—had much to do at home. Although I grew up in Iola, a Norwegian community just a few miles from the Krogwald farm, I may be deemed unworthy of my Norwegian heritage. The truth is, I am only 46 percent Norwegian. AND, I don't particularly care for lutefisk.

Lutefisk??? Uffda...No!
But Lefse? Dat's Da Way To Go!

The cooking is done.
It was so much fun!

I received a Christmas card from Berniece in December 2024. She wrote a short note (in perfect handwriting I might add), "I'm in assisted living now. Don't travel a lot but got to ND last summer to see my family. Hope to do it again this coming summer. Time will tell.

I would bet that Father Time will tell her to have a great time!

FROM ART SCHOOL
TO ASPEN
(And Beyond)!

Aspen, Colorado: a beautiful ski town, home today to four great ski mountains as well as hundreds of back-country trails and slopes, upscale lodges and restaurants, and countless celebrities. One of them, the late singer/song writer, John Denver, penned many of his songs of and about the area, including "Starwood of Aspen" (his home on the cliff across the Roaring Fork River in the western outskirts of Aspen) overlooking the mountains he loved to ski.

> And I tell you I'm happy to be here
> To share and consider this time
> For I see here the shadows of changes
> And a feeling of new friends to find.

Kathleen Butterworth Wilson found her new home and new friends in Aspen also, but her story begins on the East Coast.

Born in 1930 in Buffalo, New York, "Kath" was adopted by Ben and Kathleen Wyckoff Butterworth of Moline, Illinois. Kathleen's grandmother lived in Buffalo and managed the hospital where Kath was born! The Butterworths also adopted a boy they named William who lived much of his adult life in Shreveport, Louisiana and, according to Kath, was married four times.

Kath's great aunt, Katherine, was the granddaughter of John Deere, a blacksmith from Grand Detour, Illinois who invented the first "self-scouring steel plow" in 1837 and founded Deere & Company (commonly known as "John Deere"). The Fortune 500 Corporation manufactures diesel engines, agricultural machines and heavy equipment. "Nothing runs like a Deere."

In 1948 Deere moved his successful business 70 miles southeast to Moline, IL (located in the "Quad City Metropolitan Area" that includes

East Moline and Rock Island in Illinois as well as Davenport and Bettendorf in Iowa).

Kath's great uncle, William Butterworth, became President of the company in 1912 after serving as its Treasurer for many years. "Uncle Will" and his family lived in their *Hillcrest* home on "Millionaire Row" built by John Deere and given to his daughter for a wedding present. The restored family home in Grand Detour is listed on the National Register of Historic Places. Butterworth died when Kath was six years old.

It was no accident that Kath became interested in art history. Her great aunt, a large and rather stout lady who always wore lace dresses and resembled Queen Victoria, was a friend of an art dealer. The ceiling in her spacious home came from a Venice palace—delivered from Italy in three sections!

Beginning early in her life, Kath was exposed to the finer things in life, meeting influential people, traveling, and attending the best schools. Kath was, what we called, a "tomboy." Some of her finer things in life were playing marbles, football, and skiing on neighborhood snow bumps they call "hills." There was a drainage stream in back of their house. "Let's make a swimming pool," Kath suggested to her friends, and they built a dam. Here the kids swam for a month or so before the city realized the drainage wasn't coming through! The dam was so well made that they had to dynamite it loose! Kath reminisces, "And we had to work the rest of the year to pay for that!"

Kath also remembers being "kicked out of Brownies" (an organization for younger girls prior to becoming Girl Scouts) because she wouldn't make or play with paper dolls.

Kath speaks of "lots of wonderful memories" such as visiting her grandmother who summered in East River, New York. She also spent time at "fabulous Fishers Island" where, at age seven or eight, she played marbles with Admiral "Bull" Halsey (a retired chief admiral of the Pacific Fleet in World War II).

[Note: Fishers Island is a 9-mile x 1-mile island located at the eastern end of Long Island Sound, noted for its bird, plant and marine habitat.]

While visiting her aunt and uncle in New York, Kath recalls meeting a "tall, thin man with a beak of a nose" whom she helped walk his two dogs in Gracie Park. She would later find out that man was Basil Rathbone, a South African native who was a popular Shakespearian actor in the United Kingdom and most famous in his role as Sherlock Holmes in fourteen films during the years of 1939-46.

After ninth grade, Kath attended Miss Porter's School in Farmington, Connecticut for three years. She remembers, "It was a finishing school to become a lady—and I think my mother was hopeful!"

It was here that she met a transfer student, Inger, from Norway. They became close friends. Kath would later visit Inger and her husband, Haakon, in Norway at their family home in Oslo. She spent time at their summer home in Gola as well. Haakon ran the largest bakery in Oslo and was baker for the King of Norway.

Kath also met Jacqueline Bouvier at Farmington. They were in a Spanish class together. "We found out we would get A's," Kath recalls, "if we made up tales of romance—the sadder, the better!" "Jackie," a national champion horseback rider, invited Kath (and she accepted) to go riding with her. After Farmington, they went their separate ways. Later in life they talked about "finding any strengths" in their respective son's educational challenges. Kath recalls a letter from Jackie reminding her. "Remember, you were going to go riding with me." Both women went on with their busy lives, however, and a riding date never materialized. Of course, Jackie went on to marry senator John F. Kennedy and in 1961 became First Lady of the United States.

While in her junior year at Farmington, the history class went to the United Nations where Kath attended a presentation by humanitarian, women's rights activist and former First Lady, Eleanor Roosevelt. (President Roosevelt married his distant cousin with the same last name.) Eleanor queried the young women, asking for their thoughts and goals. During her senior year, Kath would meet Eleanor again. Eleanor still remembered Kath's interest in art history!

Kath went on to pursue that interest at Mills College in Oakland, California, with thoughts of working at an art gallery San Francisco. Turns out, the open positions there didn't pay well, and living expenses were high.

While in college, Kath further developed her interest in skiing. She made her first trip to Aspen in 1952. It was on this Aspen trip that she met Waddell ("Waddy") Catchings who ran the Roaring Fork dormitory. He offered her a job at his place of business—it was an invitation that Kath kept in the back of her mind!

Upon graduation from Mills, her parents gave Kath a one-month trip with John Jay Ski Tours to Austria, Switzerland and Italy. Jay had put aside a writing position at Time, Inc. and a scholarship to Oxford College in England to ski and to eventually become a legendary ski-film maker. Marsha, a friend from college, was Kath's roommate on the ski trip.

After returning from the European ski trip, Kath returned to Aspen, Colorado to resume her ski-bum status. (By this time, and at this location, emphasis was more on "ski" than "bum.") She began work in the cafeteria, then as a desk clerk at Roaring Fork. Catchings offered her a free dinner if the cash register came out even!

In Aspen, Kath was known as "Katy." It gets confusing with Kathy, Kathleen, Kathryn...but we will continue to call her "Kath!"

Being a ski bum was not all play in the snow. Kath would head to the slopes every morning. In the afternoon she visited businesses in Aspen to get news on their sales, events, etc. that she would list in the "Aspen Leaf," a daily newsletter she published along with her friend Ruth Whyte. It would become one of Kath's "most fun jobs."

Kath boiled water to raise the humidity to make the mimeograph machine work. She would print the paper, often working until late in the evening. Ruth would deliver the papers before the next morning.

Kath would add little sketches such as a St. Bernard dog with a keg on its neck with a caption underneath reading "Has anyone seen the K9 (*canine*) group? K9 is an unofficially-named mountain in the Alpine Lakes Wilderness area of Washington state. K9 was also a takeoff of a climbing group on Aspen Mountain patterned after Bob Craig's climbing group at K2-- the second highest mountain in the world after Mt. Everest, located on the borders of Pakistan and China.

Bob Craig was a good friend with whom Kath often skied. He served as CEO of the Aspen Institute from 1953-65. Bob, a renowned mountaineer who attempted to climb K2, was elected to the Mountaineering Hall of Fame in 2009. Kath met him at the Sugar Bowl Lodge in California where the ski patrollers, ski school and other employees were "snowed in" one weekend. Kath remembers sleeping on the pool table! Bob gave Kath his art books to study and hoped that she would not miss any classes. Later, they reconnected in Aspen where both were now living. Here they appeared together in an Otto Lang film, skiing arm and arm down the "Gulch." The film was cut when the two tangled up in a grand "yard sale!" (For you non-skiers, a yard sale is a bad fall with equipment and clothing scattered all around the "yard.") It was a miracle that only their pride was hurt!

Katy Starrett, another friend whom Kath had met skiing at Squaw Valley in California, leased and ran the Elbo Ranch at Moose, north of Jackson Hole, Wyoming. During the summer of 1956-67 Kath worked at Elbo, digging holes for septic tanks. Katy was a leader in turning the ranch into the Teton Science School, patterned after a science school that Bob Craig started in Breckenridge, Colorado.

Kath met world-class skiers such as Jimmy Heuga (one of only two alpine ski racers at that time to win an Olympic medal in his sport), Art Devlin (Olympic ski jumper), and Gladys "Skeeter" Werner, (youngest member of the U.S. ski team at the 1954 World Championships). Skeeter became Kath's roommate.

Kath raced in the Harriman Cup in Sun Valley, Idaho. It was here that she also made her debut in ski jumping! Jerryann Devlin, Art Devlin's sister and a competitive skier in her own right, had a few beers with Kath between their first and second slalom runs. With a "buzz on," Jerryann suggested they try the Ruud Mountain jump. Art made sure they climbed high enough on the mountain to not land on the flat of the outrun. That probably prevented a potential serious injury as both Jerryann and Kath took quite a tumble upon landing (another "yard sale!") The jumping experience might have been a successful one for Kath (minus the few beers and perhaps performing with *jumping*, rather than *slalom* skis).

As a little history, Averell Harriman, in 1935 chairman of the Union Pacific Railroad, partnered with an Austrian Count who had experience developing European ski resorts. The railroad was started as a means to a destination ski resort that they would develop: Sun Valley in Idaho. Here, on Ruud Mountain (named after Sigmund Ruud, famed Norwegian ski jumper) the first chairlift was built. It was a J-bar single-person lift with no back carrying skiers to the top of the 40-meter snow jump. The total endeavor was a great success!

Back to Aspen...Kath developed a friendship with the Aspen women's ski team coach, Andrea Mead Lawrence. In 1952 Andrea became the first American alpine skier to win two Olympic gold medals. Kath skied with both Andrea and husband David. The couple invited Kath and Skeeter to their Lawrence ranch where they would work, heaving heavy hay bales to build up strength needed for competitive skiing. They passed up this opportunity!

In 1954 Kath combined her skills in slalom, giant slalom and downhill racing to receive the

Bingham Cup, Aspen's women's equivalent to the prestigious Roch Cup. The races still exist.

An excerpt from December 1955 *Madamoiselle* Magazine (referring to Kath) reads:

Since she began skiing steadily in 1950, she has pulled up fast, won a national competition and a reputation for being one of the most promising young racers in America.

Barney McClean, women's coach of the U.S. Women's Alpine Ski Team, sent Kath an invitation to attend a training camp in preparation for the 1956 Olympics. Kath never got the invitation. "I personally addressed it and mailed it to you," he explained. Instead of being delivered, and for some unknown reason, the letter was held at the Aspen Post Office.

There were tryouts in Stowe, Vermont as well, but Kath hadn't received the required training. However, she continued to have a lot of fun in Aspen. Soon she became an instructor with the Aspen ski school.

Kath was working for a real estate agency in Aspen, owned some land there and was planning to open a photography shop with the legendary Dick and Miggs Durrance. Dick was a seventeen-time national champion alpine ski racer who married a ski racer (Miggs). She was named an alternate on the U.S. Olympic Ski Team after only two years of ski experience. Both later became nationally renowned photographers.

Kath went home to Moline during the summer of 1956 to attend a wedding. Groom-to-be Bud had a plan for Kath. He wanted to "fix her up" with a friend in his wedding party. The friend, "Chuz," and Kath actually met the day before the wedding, without help from the groom, and "clicked." Chuz had a date with another gal, but took her home after telling his mother "not to let Kath out of the door!" He was back in record time!

Kath's father drove back to Aspen with her. At a stop along the way, he pulled out a bottle of Bourbon and offered Kath a drink. She was a Scotch drinker, but accepted anyway.

"Well, you gonna marry the bastard?"

"I think so, Dad." Nothing else was said during the whole trip!

Chuz proposed on Kath's birthday: December 27, 1956. They were married June 8, 1957.

Chuz was not a skier. Kath put him in lessons at Aspen. He learned "because he had to!" He did play tennis though. Chuz and Kath both took lessons with Gardnar Mulloy, ranked No. 1 U. S.

player in 1952 and later inducted into the International Tennis Hall of Fame. They also spent a week at John Newcombe's tennis camp in Braunfels, Texas where, as Kath puts it, "they worked our buns off." I'm sure Kath thought it worthwhile—as long as she could indulge in the "eye candy" provided by Newcombe! Kath later entered club tournaments in Florida, adding another skill to her long list of accomplishments.

Chuz, born and raised in Rock Island, Illinois, became Chairman of the 1st National Bank of the Quad Cities, President of the Rock Island Chamber of Commerce and President of the Illinois Bank Association. The couple would adopt three children. Today, Clinton lives in Naples, Florida. Charlie is at home with Kath in northern Wisconsin and Katy lives in Rock Island, Illinois. Chuz passed away on December 29, 2020.

10th Mountain Division

The U.S. Army 10th Mountain Division
was created to engage in defense of the
New England states against possible attack.

Recruits in the specialized elite mountain warfare unit trained at Camp Hale in the Colorado Rocky Mountains. Here they would develop, or further develop, skills like skiing and rock climbing while carrying 90-lb. backpacks and surviving overnight in temperatures well below zero. This location was chosen because a railroad passed through the area and the valley was large enough to house 18,000 Army recruits. Accomplished skiers and back-country adventurers from other countries, as well as those in the U.S., enlisted.

While "The 10th" never saw action in the United States during World War II, they were active in

Europe. Their most well-known conquests took place on Riva Ridge and Mt. Belvedere in northern Italy. Lt. Col. Earl Clark (they called him "Lt. Piccolo" or "Little Lieutenant") remembered: "I weighed 118 lbs. and could hardly lift the backpacks off the floor." (Eventually they were lightened.) Clark also described the 7-1/2 ft. hickory skis. "The original skis didn't even have metal edges...but they corrected that."

The German Gothic Line (Gotenstellung) was a defense border eight miles deep and 108 miles wide, across the Triennial coast midway over the Apennine Mountains, shown on maps as a reversed S curve, to the Adriatic coast.

The Germans had an advantage of rolling hills and valleys on their side of the range. From their ridge-top encampment they would look over a 2,000-foot steep cliff. This seemed to assure the Nazis that they had secured a position of protection from any major assaults.

However, on the night of February 18, 1945, Earl Clark led his company of 700 soldiers, armed with ropes, pitons, anchors, grenades and their rifles scaled cliffs to Riva Ridge and caught the Germans by surprise.

While U.S. soldiers were slowly advancing up the steep mountain, liaison engineers were building a tram line and a 1,500-foot funicular lift to transport supplies as well as to bring dead and injured soldiers down (including Germans). An unexpected fog set in, concealing their positions. Spotlights from the base reflected off the clouds, providing better vision on the hazardous climb. The American troops surprised the Germans with hand grenades as they were awakening that morning. The fight lasted five days; 17 Americans were killed.

The day after the Riva Ridge assault, 13,000 men climbed nearby Mt. Belvedere and took control after two or three weeks.

Platoon leader Hugh Evans watched his good friend Bob Fisher, die in his arms on top of Belvedere. Enraged, Evans moved forward to where the gunfire originated. Ignoring his own safety, he killed eight enemy soldiers and helped capture over twenty more. He would later receive a Silver Star medal for his accomplishments that day, and would also receive a Bronze Star and a Purple Heart medal during his tour of duty. (Kath was best friend of Hugh's bride and a bridesmaid at their wedding after the war. She had dated Hugh's brother for a couple of years back in her college days.)

During the next several weeks, the 10th pushed north, battling through Bologna and fiercely across the Po River to Lake Gorda. They liberated many small Italian towns and also captured Benito Mussolini's headquarters and villa.

Close to 1,000 ski soldiers were killed and over 4,000 wounded while fighting in the Apennine mountains in 1945.

The 10th was called back to the United States in July to prepare for an expected Japanese invasion, but Japan surrendered on August 15, 1945. Members of a newer 10th are still being deployed however—in countries such as Iraq, Afghanistan, Pakistan and Syria.

After the war about 500 foreign-born soldiers obtained U. S. citizenship. About 250 soldiers from the 10th (both foreign born and those from the U.S.) began building ski resorts throughout the United States. The ski industry now huge, continues to expand to this day.

Vail ski resort in Colorado named their longest ski run Riva Ridge. (Other resorts included the name as well.) Back-country huts near Aspen, Vail and other nearby ski areas were built from donations from the 10th Foundation as well as others. Architect Fritz Benedict, a veteran of the 10th Mountain Division, oversaw the project. The huts served as overnight stops for "hut hikes" that became increasingly popular.

Hugh Evans became President of the 10th, made up of former military men. After skiing on a couple of 10th hut trips, Kath was named "the camp follower." She petitioned the "higher-ups" to let her become an Associate Member of the 10th. Evans replied in a letter: "My dear, how can I possibly refuse when the leaders of the 10th want you to be a member?"

Kath joined her friends in the 10th on hikes to all but one of the seventeen (at the time) 10th-operated back-country huts in the Colorado Rockies. Sometimes the outings would take them to two or three huts. Kath recalled the Eiseman hut near Vail as "a terrible climb." They carried 35-lb. back packs, sleeping bags, food and equipment. Kath was the only woman on most of the hut hikes

Chuz, also an Associate Member, made only one hut trip in 2008 near Vail. Due to respiratory problems, it would be his only mountain excursion with the 10th.

Today 350 miles of trails connect the huts. Some are privately owned, scattered from near Aspen to Breckenridge, to Vail--and one near Winter Park. They vary in size; one has sixteen beds! The warmth of the huts, abundance of good wine and the memories of those who served in WWII bring out little-known stories that will never be forgotten.

The Colorado Hut Association name honors the men who served in the 10th Mountain Division of the U.S. Army. There is a special bond amongst members. Few who battled at Riva Ridge/Mt. Belvedere are still alive. Others, like Kath, are Associate Members—all self-reliant men and women who share a great love of the outdoors, a spirit inherent in their pursuit of excellence, and enjoyment of camaraderie.

The veterans retain and relive memories...such as when Earl Clark, who learned to ski at southern Wisconsin's Wilmot Mountain (well, really just a "hill") found a cache of good French champagne and brandy in a huge building in the town of Riva del Garda just after the Germans had surrendered. A general, Mark Clark (no relation to Earl), ordered the 10th to send it back to his headquarters. Earl told them, "Sorry, it was all gone." Actually, a couple of the bottles were brought to a reunion in Italy in 2006!

One night, while relaxing in a hut, Hugh relived the day up on Riva Ridge when his buddy was killed by the Germans:

> We were in a foxhole for two weeks, then sent behind the lines to a hill town Montecatini for R&R, and finally back to the foxhole. That's when Hugh said it was at least 90% anger--the rest stupidity and maybe some courage— storms ahead and single-handedly wiped out three machine gun emplacements. His best friend and foxhole partner had just died in his arms from shrapnel hitting the trees that were partially left standing.

Hugh's wife, Ann, had never heard the story before. Kath remembers, "There was a lot of wine consumed that night in the 10th," and maybe a few tears!

Kath made her last hut trip in the mid 1990s, but the memories today are as vivid as ever. Most of her friends from the 10th have passed away--Hugh Evans at age 97, Earl Clark at age 95. Art Devlin, a B-24 pilot, though not a member of the 10th, received three Purple Heart medals and other military honors. He passed away in April 2004 at age 81.

[For a descriptive, dramatic and in-depth story of our country's first mountain soldiers and their

place in conquering the Nazis during World War II in Europe, read THE LAST RIDGE by McKay Jenkins.

Today, at age 93, Kath looks forward to downhill skiing with her friends every Wednesday at Powderhorn Mountain near Bessemer, Michigan and biking various trails (both activities with the Northwoods Ski Touring Association club out of nearby Minocqua). She enjoys kayaking and hiking in warmer weather. She still cross-country skis and snowshoes. She is active in various clubs and associations, walks her two dogs daily, works out regularly at the local Mac (Manitowish Athletic Club), lifts weights and does other exercises via Zoom in her home.

Her more passive side might find Kath working on one of her many miniature replicas of places she remembers fondly--like her living room in Moline. Everything is put together on a scale of 12:1. Items are either purchased or hand made. An example of her creativity is shown in her southwestern adobe home. The landscaped exterior consists of coffee grounds—used for flowers and rose bushes. How's that for creativity!

It all started in a miniature shop located in Highland Park, Illinois. Brooke Tucker, an actress who appeared in Charlie's Angels and Ghost Busters, walked in to the store and became fascinated with the subject—later became a "guru" in the miniature world and offered seminars. Kath attended one such seminar in Bonita Springs, Florida. They talked about their dads: both were the same age, same build, wore a mustache, liked the same things, and died at age 65 of cancer! Kath's dad owned various foundries. Brooke's dad, Forest, was an actor—both on stage and in the movies, appearing with stars such as Charlton Heston and Gary Cooper.

Kath shows off one of her miniatures at a presentation at a local library.

Kath belongs to a craft club where she knits, does needlepoint and chit-chats with fellow members. She admits that she finds it hard not to make errors when knitting and talking at the same time!

She has worked with disadvantaged kids at schools and helped with auditory programs. She volunteers at her church, helping with their annual August Fleazaar program (a very large "yard sale" of a different type), with planning, organizing, and collecting items beginning in May each year. Kath mentioned that she usually has Mondays free "from nine a.m. on--and rainy days as well."

While Kath's young adult years could be a transition from a period of art--surrounding and introduced to her, and her graduation from college with an art degree—to a great skier with many experiences meeting famous skiers and competing in the United States as well as in various European countries. Today, it's been years since she skied in Aspen. In a manner of speaking, it's been "From Art to Aspen," now "Aspen to Art," and she adds "and Beyond!" Skiing, however, is still an important and enjoyable part of her life.

In 2018, while downhill skiing at Whitefish, Montana with other members of NASTA, Kath took her first run of the day using rental skis. She didn't like the skis and was on her way down the mountain to exchange them for another pair. She fell, knocked herself out, and broke her hip. She survived the week, unable to ski. It was a long train trip home! Kath talks about her "fake hip," but still gets around pretty well!

During autumn 2023, Kath visited the Utah canyons on a Roads Scholar trip (and also spent a week volunteering at Best Friends Animal Sanctuary in Angel Canyon--that Kath describes as "one of the most beautiful places I've seen!") There were a lot of hikes, some in higher elevations. Once a long-distance runner, Kath continues to be a strong hiker. The steep inclines on some of these hikes, however, resulted in a lingering sore leg. Sitting in her easy chair, Kath remarked, "I'm resting my leg." Yet, she is ready for the next adventure.

When asked if she had any regrets regarding her life, Kath replied that she had only one! She had gone to Sorrento, Italy one summer with Marsha Sehm, a friend from Peoria, Illinois whom she had met in Aspen. They left in early February and came back just before Christmas. "We had room and board for $2/day. We had a huge room with a nice view and covered with arbor vines where breakfast was served." They got to know a newspaper publisher from Kentucky. He and his wife invited the two gals to join them for two weeks on a yacht owned by our ambassador to Greece. (The ambassador's two children could not join them, so there was room on the yacht.) Marsha had met a young man in the U.S. Army and was anxious to see him. Kath and Marsha were traveling by car together, so it was an offer Kath felt she must turn down.

A review of just one of Kath's photo albums contained pictures taken in Europe--mostly of handsome, hunky members of the male species. There was Alden, Bill, (two) Bobs, Cardo, Carlino, Christian, Chuck, Dave, Dean, Dick, Eddie, Eric, Frank, Franz, Fred, Hank, Hans, Jack, Jake, Jim, Joe, John, Joseph, Ken, Jean, Jerry, Jesse, Lauren, Les, Lou, Luigi, Mark, Marrion, Marsh, Mason, Max, Michael, Neil, Pardo, Pete, Pietro, Ralph, "Red," Rick, Roger, Ross, "Shady" (last name: Lane), "Red," Sepp, Sidney, Skip, Stan, Steve, Ted, Tony, Tim, Waddell, Willy and "Windy". That's sixty sexy men: count them! Maybe her heart was racing...as well as her skis!

Chuz, after meeting many of Kath's old friends, acted a bit perturbed! "Didn't you ever ski with any women?"

Kath has lived a life that many could only dream about. Most of us have many regrets of things we wished we would have done differently and would be totally envious of the life of Kath Wilson. Life's experiences and rewards were not handed to her on a platter, but the results of hard work, drive, passion, inner strength, attitude and will.

Kath had a busy week rehearsing for an upcoming Christmas production put on by a local theater group, helping to decorate her church for the upcoming Holidays, and then heading to Moline to visit friends and family. She is like the Energizer Bunny, a pink mechanical rabbit wearing sunglasses and beating a drum. Developed in 1988 to advertise Energizer batteries, the bunny "keeps going and going and going..."

As of late 2022, the oldest known downhill skier was 105-year-old George Jedenhoff who lives in Utah. Stick around another decade: The next such record holder could be Kathleen Wilson! (Note: George turned 107 in July 2024. Reports say he finally hung up his skis!)

Shown below is Kath at her log home on Harris Lake in Winchester, Wisconsin, which she and Chuz built in 1999 after falling in love with Wisconsin's Northwoods. Living with her today are her son Charlie and two loving labradors, Callie and Maia.

She walks her dogs every afternoon. The time is 1 p.m. and Maia has started pacing up and down—she knows it's getting close to her exercise time! It's time for me to leave Kath's house; I conclude the interview--exhausted just listening to her talk about all of her accomplishments and activities!

Note the dumbbell on the floor next to the chair. (The "smart belle" exercises even while sitting!

TAKE ME OUT TO
THE BALL GAME

So, let's root, root, root for the home team
If they don't win, it's a shame
For it's one, two, three strikes you're out
at the old ball game

(A verse from the song Take Me Out to the Ballgame
by Jack Norworth and Albert von Tilzer)

The subject of this story is Dolores Koechel Thiel, Sheboygan, Wisconsin native and ardent baseball fan.

The home team, "Chairmakers," was a semi-pro baseball club that was based in Sheboygan from the late 1800s through the 1930s.

Dolores' son, Wally Thiel, who continues to research baseball in this area for an upcoming book, explains:

Back around the turn of the 20th century Sheboygan had a heavy industrial base, much of it dedicated to the manufacture of furniture--including A LOT of chairs. Crocker Chair and Phoenix Chair were among the prominent firms. As the local team traveled to other cities within the league, they began to be referred to as the "Chairmakers," or just the "Chairs."

The name of the team was changed to the Sheboygan Indians during the 1940s, and they became a minor league team affiliated with the Brooklyn Dodgers.

Dolores was born June 21, 1926, the youngest of three children, to parents Frank and Meta Koechel. She was an outgoing child, curious and comfortable around people of all ages.

The family lived adjacent to the North Side Athletic Park, home to the Chairmakers. Separated from the Park only by their garden, the family would find "foul balls"—hidden amongst the carrots, tomatoes, beans and raspberries! The baseballs were then traded back to the team in exchange for free admission tickets to their home games!

It was the evening of July 2, 1937. The Chairs were hosting an exhibition game with the Kansas City Monarchs, a dominant team from the Negro American League. The legendary Monarchs "swamped" the local team that evening; the final score was 20-4. Dolores, eleven years old at the time, scored her own *home run* with an event of a lifetime!

That evening amiable Dolores, armed with a free pass and her little red autograph book, walked over to the ballpark to cheer on her team! She sat with a few of her neighborhood friends and their parents. The pre-teen had made friends with team members and often sat with their wives as well. (Though a lot of baseballs ended up on the Koechel's property, obviously not all family members could have passes for every game! It was Dolores' turn to "root" for the home team!)

Nobody seems sure of how the autograph book got into the hands of the Monarchs that July second. When Dolores came home that night, she had autographs of J. L. Wilkinson, Andy Cooper, Willard Brown and "Bullet" Rogan. All of these remarkable men would end up as members of the National Baseball Hall of Fame in Cooperstown, New York!

J. Leslie Wilkinson (a Caucasian; no first name) was an American sports executive who founded the Des Moines, Iowa All Nations baseball team in 1912, It was the first racially and culturally integrated team in the league. The team moved to Kansas City in 1915. In 1920 Wilkinson built the Monarchs, recruiting the best players from the All Nations team as well as from another all-black U.S. Army team.

Andy Cooper, left-handed pitcher whose nickname was "Lefty," perfected the fastball, curveball and screwball—and seemingly knew the weaknesses of every batter in the league! He later became manager of the Monarchs and led them to three pennants from 1937 to 1940.

Willard "Home Run" Brown was a power hitter, a speedy outfielder who finished his career with an impressive .347 batting average.

Charles Wilber Rogan (nickname: Bullet) was a pitcher, an outfielder, AND a great hitter—a bit unusual for a pitcher. He later worked as an umpire in the Negro American League. Rogan was inducted into the Hall of Fame in 1998. Wilkinson, Cooper and Brown made their debut in 2006. The Negro leagues were recognized as "major leagues" in December 2020.

Autographs of these great players on baseballs or legal documents today can be worth "a pretty penny." Make that "dollar(s)." The signatures in Dolores red autograph book, however, are priceless in memories!

Over time many of the Negro league players integrated into the National or American Leagues. The quality of the Negro leagues diminished as their players were drafted into what was previously all-white leagues. By 1952 the Negro leagues had faded into history.

Back to Dolores: She attended Jefferson Elementary and graduated from Sheboygan North High School in 1944.

High School Grad

Two years out of high school, Dolores married Walter Thiel. Pastor E. R. Kroeger of the St. John's E&R Church, who had baptized and confirmed Dolores, now pronounced the couple "man and wife."

The Thiels had three sons. All played baseball and became enthusiastic fans of the sport—a *triple play*!

Wally recalls his mom making a baseball suit for him when he was five or six years old. He proudly wore the gray flannel suit to home ball games. Although Wally doesn't remember what happened to that boyhood suit, his grandfather's circa 1908 baseball uniform still hangs in his closet today!

As mentioned, (now retired) son Wally has become an author and is currently working with the Sheboygan City Historical Research Center, delving deeper into the era starting with the formation of the National League in 1876 and continuing with the American League that was created at the turn of the 20th century. It has been an interesting six years of progress, researching and finally putting it all on paper. The proverbial "light at the end of the tunnel" is now visible!

On her 85th birthday a joyous Dolores accompanied her three sons to Milwaukee to see the Brewers defeat the visiting Tampa Bay Rays. The Brewers went on to win their first ever National League Central title that year.

Dolores was a remarkable woman, "always up for anything." She gave her boys the opportunity to be the men they wanted to become and encouraged them to take the chances they needed to get there.

Dolores Thiel
Over the fence, but never "over the hill"

Dolores' love of life, love of baseball, and love for her three amazing sons who shared that passion, could be defined as her own *grand slam*! As for the little red autograph book: it's in a safe place and will probably be passed on to the next generation.

Dolores' husband, Walter, passed away in 1990. Dolores followed him three decades later, on June 2, 2022. She was 95 years of age.

RELATIVELY SPEAKING

I want to include Lois L'Hommedieu Seward Christopher in this book. Lois married my first cousin, Bernard ("Bernie") Seward, who grew up near Oconto Falls, WI. Lois was born in Ohio on February 12, 1925, but later moved to Florida.

Lois received a teaching degree from Wheaton College Academy in Illinois in 1942. In 1948 she received a degree in religion from Florida

Southern College and was awarded the Walter L. Harris medal in Theology. After one year serving as Youth Director of the First Methodist Church in Ocala, Florida, she spent the rest of her career teaching in St. Petersburg and then Key West, Florida.

Lois found herself teaching at a Title 1 school, working with students with discipline and general apathy problems. She describes her frustration:

> Many of my students just did not see the need for education when their fathers were getting rich just by using their fishing boats to bring in "square grouper" (a term they used for drugs) from Cuba. I had always loved teaching but I slowly had been losing my enthusiasm for trying to get through to students who simply did not want to learn.

Lois retired in 1980 at age 55.

Within just one week of retiring, Lois pursued her long-time goal of becoming a Licensed Unity teacher, graduating from the Unity School of Christianity.

One of the principles of the Unity Church is "You can always begin again." She taught religion first in Key West, and later at Christ Church Unity in Orlando where she served for 30 years!

In 1996 (at age 71) she completed her Master's Degree in Counselor Education at the University of Central Florida!

Lois met her first husband (my first cousin), Bernard Seward, at a dance. He was in the U.S. Air Force. They married in 1952 and had two sons, Bernard Jr. (Buck) and David.

In 1960 the young family moved to Key West, Florida where Bernie had just started a job at the Weather Bureau. It was one of the first stations to use radar to predict weather.

In late summer of that year Hurricane Donna hit the Keys. Bernie took Lois to the new radar tower to see the approaching storm. It was the first time ever to view and react to hurricanes in this manner. This promised to be a dangerous storm!

There was no time to evacuate the two-lane highway leading from their island to the mainland; no time to put up storm shutters. Lois and their two sons spent the night with a neighbor, a woman who also had two young sons. Electricity was out, telephone lines were down, communication by any means was impossible. By morning the worst was over; the kids slept through the ordeal.

Key West had suffered damage but, as it turned out, they were on the "weaker side of the storm." The Middle Keys, however, were not as lucky. Bridges were washed out, refrigerators and furniture adorned trees left standing. The island of Marathon was under eight feet of water! That night 354 people lost their lives. Key West was cut off from the mainland for two months. The U.S. Navy brought in food and water, rationed only so much per person.

Before the storm hit, Bernie and Lois had filled their boat with water to keep it from blowing away! That would now serve as a source of water to wash their cloth diapers and to be able to flush the toilet!

In future years many other hurricanes would hit Florida's tip. In 1966 it was Hurricane Inez. This was the first time since 1919 that a hurricane's "eye" would pass directly over the island. Lois remembered it well!

> Mother and I sat out on the porch for a while listening to the radio, watching cars go by, and swatting mosquitoes (there were millions of them), The weather bureau said the winds were only 3 mph. The radio kept warning people to stay in off the street as when the storm hit us again, it would be stronger than ever. Reports kept coming in from the Keys of 100-140 mile-per-hour winds. We never

saw anything like it. The varying 15- to 35-mile-wide storm center lingered two hours and 45 minutes.

Then about 9:30 p.m., Lois recalled, "all hell broke loose." Metal flew off nearby roofs. High-tension wires lit up." Then, all was dark. The storm sounded like a "freight train" or "low-flying jet planes."

Houses in Key West were strongly built; the Seward's house survived the storm with little damage. Their boat ended up on the opposite side of the canal abutting their property but suffered little damage. Their neighbor's boat, however, ended up on the bottom of the canal.

There were other things to fear in Key West besides hurricanes. One morning the Sewards awoke to sounds of planes from the mainland continually arriving at the airport just a mile from their home. Just 90 miles from Key West lies Cuba, a communist nation with strong ties to Russia. There was no trading with Cuba; the Cold War was on. U.S. spy planes had spotted nuclear missiles in Cuba, posing a new danger to the Keys. President Kennedy had ordered a naval blockade. There was strong fear of an imminent attack. Barbed-wire fences were erected directly in front of the Weather Bureau; missiles were being put in place. Fear enveloped the island.

Talks between President Kennedy and Russian leader Khrushchev seemed to be at a standstill, but after 13 days an agreement was reached. Missiles were dismantled; troops were leaving. Residents were grateful and thankful.

In time Bernie retired and spent time with school children relating the dangers of lightening. Lois had been afraid of lightening since a child when she and her sister "saw a streak of lightening run up the limb of the tree right to our bedroom window." The strike had burned away the tree limb. The family felt fortunate that the bolt had not set their house on fire.

Lois and Bernie had moved from Key West to central Florida. One sunny afternoon, as they headed up the inter-coastal waterway toward Melbourne, they encountered a very strong thunderstorm. There was no way to get to land; they were in a deep channel following markers indicating shallow water.

Rain became so heavy that the couple could no longer see the markers from the "flying bridge" on top the boat. So, they moved down to the cabin to read a chart defining where the markers were located. Lightening was in the water all around the boat. Lois said a short prayer and then concentrated on directing the captain, Bernie—one marker at a time. As fast as the storm arrived, it moved on. Soon, the sun came out.

Lois felt that "fear takes a back seat" when a task on hand needs to be done. She advises us to remember: "All you need is a plan. Stay on the markers, follow the chart, and have the courage to press on to your destination." Good advice-- whether lost in a storm or living your life!

Bernie had a major heart attack during his first year of retirement. He was also an asthmatic. A few years later, in 1990, Bernie passed away at the age of sixty.

Lois devoted herself to her work as a licensed teacher in the Unity Church. She found this to be very fulfilling, but there was little time for a social life. After a few years she felt she wanted another meaningful relationship. She sat down a wrote a list of qualities that she would look for in a prospective mate:

- Good moral character
- Sense of humor
- Positive attitude
- Liking to travel
- Shared Unity Church belief systems

The last quality turned out to be the first one on her list when she met and married her second husband, Jim Christopher.

Lois talked with a friend who had a common interest in dancing. They decided to enroll in dance class. Soon they had enough courage to go to weekly senior dances in the area. Here they hoped to meet a nice gentleman or two for dance partners—but maybe even to get into dating a bit. It took quite a while, but Lois would not let herself be discouraged.

Then, one night, Lois was introduced to Jim. He wanted to learn a new dance step; she readily volunteered. Soon they were taking up country dancing and having a lot of fun together. Jim belonged to the Church of Christ but began to worship with Lois and soon became a member of the Unity Church.

One morning Jim came to Lois' house to ask her to go to lunch. She wasn't home. He left a message that he would call later. Lois finally called Jim, but the calls went unanswered. She then tried his son and got the bad news. Jim had suffered a stroke and was recovering from surgery. The prognosis wasn't good; a second brain surgery was required.

Friends urged Lois to move on. Today the advice often is: "You don't want to be a nurse or a purse." But Lois found a new purpose. "I knew I loved him and wanted to do everything in my power to help him return to his life."

Lois visited Jim at the rehab center almost every day. She brought him a radio so he could listen to the dance music they both loved. She talked to him, not knowing at times if he heard or understood.

Soon Jim was in physical therapy, learning to walk again: from his wheel chair to a walker, and then dancing a few steps with Lois as she supported him.

Jim was staying with his son and wife now, in Deltona. Lois was driving down from Orlando two or three times a week. It became difficult, both physically and mentally. Soon she was welcomed in to live at the Christopher household. Lois sold her large condo. This greatly eased her mind with the increased cash flow and decreased responsibilities.

Jim had some setbacks. Just beginning to walk without a walker, he fell and broke a hip. Some time later he fell out of his wheelchair and broke the other hip. But he never gave up!

Despite Jim's remaining handicaps, he and Lois were able to travel to Massachusetts, North Carolina, Hawaii, the Virgin Islands and the Bahamas. They visited Key West and enjoyed a helicopter ride over central Florida.

Jim passed away in 2009. When I started to communicate with Lois, mainly by Christmas letters each year, I found out that she was the author of two books, "Life Begins at 70," and "WHAT are you AFRAID of?"

Lois, now in her mid-90s, had formed a group that met in her home. Her first book was written to help group members, mostly under 70 years of age, to meet the problems of growing older.

Her second book dealt with some of her own fears. A few of them were discussed in this chapter: Fear of lightening, of natural disasters, attack, war, snakes, epidemics, illness, and even fear of the unknown worries her. She worried if she would ever find a husband and have children.

As a child, Lois developed a fear of fire. Eating her breakfast alone in the kitchen, she suddenly saw smoke and flames erupt from their stovepipe. Lois called out to her mother in an adjacent room who beat the fire with a broom. She then poured water on the remaining embers. The fire was extinguished before it spread, but they worried about it happening again.

At age five, Lois' parents took her to a "town swimming hole." It was a hot day in July, and they hoped to "get cooled off." Lois played in the shallow water as her parents watched. She wandered just a little too far, and a strong current started to carry her away. Her dad saw her go under once, twice, and after the third time was able to pull her out of the water.

Lois had another such experience at age nine when she was carried by a rip tide; again, her father was able to come to the rescue!

Seems bad things can come in threes! As a ten-year-old, and playing with a boy her own age in the woods, they came upon a small dam. The water was only a few inches deep at the top. However, Lois lost her footing and fell into deep water over the dam. Her playmate jumped in and pulled her to safety!

The next, and obvious step, was swimming lessons!

Other fears that possessed Lois also were results of her life experiences. Lois was attending St. Petersburg Junior College (the third college she had attended in one semester)! Rather than walk several blocks, she chose a path through a wooded area to avoid being late for class. She heard someone running behind her. Suddenly, the man grabbed her and punched her in the jaw, breaking four teeth, including two molars. One molar was shattered in seven pieces! The perpetrator knocked her to the ground and started ripping at her clothes. He stopped suddenly after hearing someone else coming up the path, taking her purse and running away.

The man who attacked her was never apprehended.

At one point, during the summer after her first year at college, panic attacks were controlling her life. She would develop shakes, fear of crowds, noises, and going anywhere by herself. At times Lois believed she was having a heart attack as her heart was beating rapidly. It took a second doctor to ask if she had been through any recent traumatic experiences. Of course, she had! Less than a year ago she had been the victim of an assault and attempted rape! Because she had gone right back to the stresses of college and attempted to stuff the terrible experience within and go on wither her life, it had resulted in the nervous reactions. The kind and patient doctor enabled Lois to return to a normal life.

Lois wrote in her book, "The most important way that I've handled fear is by my faith in God, and trust in His direction and protection. And I've never known it to fail. Truly I have been blessed."

Lois passed away in June 2023 at age 98. Tributes to her include "dear, sweet soul," "great and loving person" and person of "sincerity and kindness." She had a purpose of helping others. She found her strength in the Bible, her faith in God, and the Unity Church.

GRAMMA LEMIRANDE

Emma Shemick was born in Cooperstown, Wisconsin on September 23, 1874. The Shemicks later moved to the Lena area. Emma was my maternal grandmother. I remember meeting her only a few times.

I was born in Iola, Wisconsin, where my mother, Mildred, was offered a position as a beauty operator. Mom had taken a "teacher's training" course after high school but the Great Depression hit and she couldn't find a job. So, she changed her plans and attended "beauty school" in Green Bay. She worked part time in Green Bay at a shop owned by a friend she met in school. She made $8 per week (later $10 per week) and lived in the shop owner's house. Her bedroom was a large closet; "room and board" was a part of her salary. There was very little money left over.

When she was no longer needed at the shop, her beauty school teacher called. "Millie, I have a job for you in Iola." Despite her basic shyness, she boarded a bus, suitcase in hand, and got off at the corner where her husband-to-be owned a sport shop! She rented a downtown apartment just across the street.

Mom loved to dance and dated another local man before marrying my dad, Sherman Cleaves. "Sherm," (also known as "Wimpy" after a comic book character who shared his love for hamburgers) was in his mid twenties. He had taken over the sport shop after his father died in a car accident, presumably the result of a heart attack, as he was driving back to Iola from Stevens Point where he had installed awnings that day.

Sherm learned the awning business as well. He also sold two Milwaukee papers, the *Journal* and the *Sentinel*. (I was a "paper girl" for a couple of years, delivering mainly to business locations near my dad's shop.)

The fact that he had to keep his shop open on Sunday mornings for townspeople to pick up or buy a Milwaukee paper meant that he had little time for travel. Mom never got her drivers license until she was in her mid-40s. The point of this prelude is that we didn't see much of her side of the family up in the Lena/Oconto Falls area because of the reasons mentioned.

I didn't know my grandmother well. It seems Emma Shemick Lemirande was "old" when I met her. From stories told, I got the impression that she was a strong and capable woman who dealt with hardships and saw her goals to fruition.

Emma's father, John Shemick, grew up in the Bohemian Forest near the German border of Czechoslovakia. His father was the King's Deer Herdsman. After serving eight years in the army, John immigrated to the United States

Emma attended a school in Chicago sponsored by the Singer Sewing Machine Company. There she traveled around the city on a bicycle, wearing a "bicycle suit" that she had made for herself, giving instructions and teaching sewing.

Emma came home from Chicago to visit her parents, then living near Lena, Wisconsin. Here she met Alphonse Lemirande, a neighbor not too far away from the farm she grew up on. The two soon married and had two children. With the help of a relative, Alphonse built a brick house on top of a hill where Emma gave birth to four more children. A one-room grade school with a wood-burning fireplace (but outdoor toilets) was a short walk through the nearby woods!

House that Alphonse Built

Emma had a large garden, growing everything "from ground cherries to chicory." She fed the calves and horses, cared for her children, all the while learning how to be a farmer's wife! She made all of her children's clothing, as well as items for the house—sewing, crocheting, and knitting. My mom, youngest of four girls, remembers yearning for a "store-bought" dress! Most of her clothing was handed down as the older girls outgrew them.

In the winter Al "went to work in the woods" north of Lena to earn a bit more money. Emma ran the farm and household, with some help from Al's brother who would stay with her at times.

I'm not sure if Al came home from the logging camp on weekends, or it was during a different time period, but he would transport the kids (that were old enough to attend high school in Oconto Falls), to and from by horse-drawn sleigh. On Monday mornings Emma would hand out fresh hard-boiled eggs to the kids to put in their pockets to keep their hands warm. She would send enough food, clean bedding, and whatever else was needed for the upcoming week. Al, bundled up in his warm sheepskin coat, would hitch up the horses, make sure the kids (and horses) had enough fur blankets to keep warm and do the ten-mile round trip every Monday morning and back again after school on Fridays. When spring came, or when it was too muddy, their wagon would replace the sleigh.

While Al was away, Emma ran the farm, doing the chores, milking the cows, feeding the pigs, chickens and horses. One night one of the horses got anxious for his feed and took the bottom of Emma's ear off. A doctor from five miles away came to the house and sewed the ear back on. With instructions to wash the area in warm water twice a day, Emma watched her ear heal nicely.

Al had a sudden and fatal heart attack at his home in 1936 at age 62. His only son and youngest of the six children, Harold, wanted to quit high school to help out on the farm. Emma had always insisted that all of their six children finish their high school education. And they did! She was able to manage the farm with the help of a part-time hired man.

My Gramma Lemirande passed away in 1962, a week shy of her 88th birthday. She was truly an adventurous, courageous, determined, creative, hard-working and talented woman who loved her family and did everything in her power to raise her children properly and ensure that they lead successful lives. I would like to think that I inherited some (perhaps a VERY small) portion of her admirable traits!

JOAN'S JOURNIES

Joan Tatge was born in Milwaukee, Wisconsin in May 1933 during The Great Depression. Both her mom and her dad were teachers. Joan's mom took some time away from her vocation but returned to teaching when Joan's younger brother began grade school.

As a child just beginning school in a new neighborhood, Joan made friends who shared activities: climbing trees, doing acrobatics, playing with building blocks and paper dolls, roller skating and ice skating.

Joan became aware of World War II through her uncles who visited during their furlough. Gas and food were rationed and war bond/stamps were sold. Joan recalls, "The local library acknowledged achievement for each book read by issuing a picture of a plane with a stamped bomb!" Although proud of the awards, she was beginning to learn of violence and loss of life.

During 1947-48 polio was spreading through the nation, and her neighborhood as well.

Joan came down with a mild case, luckily with no paralysis.

Now a teenager, Joan got her first job: working as a part-time secretary for Dan Hoan, candidate for Governor of Wisconsin.

In 1951 she received her high school diploma and began studies of X-ray technology at UW Madison. From 1953-1966 she worked as an X-ray/lab technician in Stoughton, Wisconsin.

Joan married Ralph Donnelly in 1954. They had three children: Karen, Michael and Brian. During this time Joan continued work at the local hospital. In 1966 Ralph, a Marine, was sent to Vietnam. The couple was now separated.

During 1966-67 Joan worked in Immunology Research at the UW Medical School. She describes 1970 as "an eventful year." Joan divorced, received her BS degree in Nursing and began working nights in Obstetrics at University Hospital until it closed in 1971.

Joan asked herself, "Now what?" With three young children she felt she needed to be home nights so applied and was hired as Public Health Nurse/Educator serving all schools and medical referrals in Dane County.

Joan married Evan Sayre, a teacher and a farmer, in 1974. Their son Benjamin was born in 1976.

In 1977 Joan and a teacher/friend decided to take a 2-1/2-week class on building a log home, held in Ely, Minnesota. Joan was fascinated. The knowledge would become important in years to come!

It is now 1978. The couple separated. Joan and son Ben moved to a nearby farm in the Madison area. Joan describes the following year as one of "pain, patience, counseling, and resignation." In 1980 Joan and Ben (now age four) moved to a lake house near Minocqua in northern Wisconsin, where they "fished and canoed, cross-country skied--and she learned to cut and stack wood."

The following year Ben began kindergarten where he exhibited learning problems. After specialist consultation in New York and an evaluation at Gunderson Clinic in La Crosse, Wisconsin, Ben was diagnosed with dyslexia and enrolled in Special Education classes at North Lakeland School near their home.

Their landlord decided to move into their rental home, so Joan and Ben rented a house on the Manitowish River. Wanting something more permanent, Joan purchased 3.94 acres in the Natural Lakes Private Preserve in the township of Presque Isle.

She returned to Minnesota in 1981 to refresh her knowledge on log-house building. Joan developed house plans, acquired permits, purchased needed tools, and located a mature stand of red pines—ready for the picking, so to speak! With the help of her instructor (who came to Wisconsin and camped on the land) and locals Ferde, Nick and later, "Ski," they built the beautiful log home on top of a hill, reached by a 150-foot driveway. The home overlooked a wooded area with abundant wildlife and quiet privacy. In spring of 1983 Joan and Ben moved into their new home! The following year Joan divorced and with her son was "free to be, you and me."

Joan felt she now had a "great job." She was employed as Human Growth and Development Coordination with Cooperative Education and Services Agency (CESA) and adjoining school districts, working on their curriculum and programs. Concurrently, she did graduate work in the field of mental health, teaching and counseling districts. Working within the northern Wisconsin school district, Joan authored, and the district was awarded, a multi-million grant!

In 1987 CESA required that Joan commute twice a week to Menomonee, Wisconsin—a 200-mile round trip. Ben bunked with family friends those days, continuing his schooling in the Northwoods.

Joan resigned, applied and was accepted to the University of Wisconsin Graduate Guidance and Counseling Program in Menomonee. She received her MS Degree in 1988 and was hired as an elementary/middle school Counselor position in Sparta, Wisconsin.

Leaving their Wisconsin log home on the hill for the school year, Joan and Ben rented an octagon museum home in West Salem. She describes the unusual home as follows.

It was a two-story home with marble-top tables in the bedroom, many more throughout the house, a winding staircase to the second floor. Despite the Old World environment, and a very old cook stove, the house was quite delightful—until cold weather came. With minimal (or no?) insulation and a questionable heating system, winter living in a museum was not a great choice. Our cat of ten years froze to death in the enclosed back porch. We discovered her an hour before leaving for one of Ben's hockey games.

One winter was enough; Joan and Ben moved out! For two weeks in the spring, they commuted from a campground. Then, they found a conventional apartment in the same West Salem school district—furnished and warm!

In June 1989 the three of them returned to the Northwoods for the summer. (There was an addition to the family—a beautiful chocolate lab puppy—a birthday gift for Ben on his 13th birthday!)

Back in West Salem for the school year, Ben was doing well in 9th grade with new friends and his hockey games. Joan, curious about overseas jobs, went to an International Job Fair in February 1991. Initially, no job offers were forthcoming. They returned to their "cabin," as Joan called it, for the summer. Natural gas became available and, along with a space heater, the log home stayed above freezing during winter months. It was no longer necessary to drain the plumbing system during their winter absence.

In 1992 Joan, still curious about overseas jobs, attended the Job Fair again. She was offered a position as School Nurse/Educator in Leysin,

Switzerland! Ben, now independent of special education and entering 11th grade, would have free education until graduation!

Joan reminisced, "After consulting with Ben and his dad, and knowing my home in the woods was always waiting, I pursued my lifetime curiosity and passion to know other cultures. Off we went...to Switzerland!"

Joan lived in a small apartment in Leysin American School in the Alps, above Lake Geneva. Ben lived nearby. His dorm was just a block up a mountain path from the Kuman Academy he attended.

Classes were canceled two afternoons a week while students/faculty skied the local mountain free of charge! (Author's note: I have Joan's white ski boots that now serve as planters for flowers in my "driftwood garden" beside my house!)

Joan coordinated health care services in two Swiss boarding schools. During spare time she and Ben "explored European art and architecture, immersed themselves in the aftermath of World War II and discovered the joy and ease of traveling in many countries."

They traveled to London, all parts of Italy, and much of eastern Europe in recovery from World War II "sobered by concentration camps, cities and countries in repair."

Ben flew home the summer of 1993 to be with his dad. In 1994 he graduated from the Leysin American School, then traveled through Europe with a classmate before returning to the United States to prepare for college. Joan returned to the Northwoods.

Two years later "Africa beckoned." Joan attended the New Orleans Job Fair and was hired as a Middle School Counselor and Life Skills Educator in Dar es Salaam, a city of over a million population, in Tanzania, East Africa!

Joan taught and counseled the natives of Tanzania and traveled throughout the continent, "becoming aware of the previous influence of the British and Germans." She went on tent safaris, "living in wild animal environments...and exploring Indian Ocean tide pools." Joan spent three weeks at Gombe National Park. Here the late Jane Goodall studied chimpanzees (members of the ape family) behavior in their natural habitat where buildings for humans are caged in and chimps roam free! She actually stayed in Goodall's home.

Near Goodall's home, the chimpanzees roam!

Joan developed curriculum At the International School of Tanganyika taught life skills to grades 7-10. She served as a faculty sponsor of the "Street Children Project" working with juniors and seniors seeking to earn their International Baccalaureate degree. Joan befriended students, promoted projects and invited them to the campus to participate in sports such as swimming and basketball. In her free time Joan traveled with another faculty member, serving as a chaperone for activities that included trips to the London theatre, holiday celebrations and spectacular athletic events.

In 1998 her contract ended. Joan, now 65, still had much more to see and do! For a while she did substitute teaching and worked part time at a variety of jobs including waitressing at a new

101

restaurant and monitoring the Natural Lakes entrance station.

In 2003 it was time for another move—this time to arctic Alaska! She worked as a Guidance Counselor in Noatak, Alaska, then in Barrow, and finally in Valdez. Joan describes this adventure as "the most challenging of all." Here she experienced "bush flying" between Eskimo villages while "learning the necessary self-subsistent life style and skills for human survival." She returned home for the summer, hoping to get in two more years in Alaska for retirement eligibility. However, it was not to be.

While hauling wood in her wheel barrow, Joan shifted her weight and fell, resulting in a broken back. After exploratory surgery at that time, she had continuous post-operative "horrid pain." In December 2010 the surgeon did a bone graft from her hip to her spine to replace a missing disc.

While recovering, a friend suggested Joan spend the winter with her in Puerto Vallarta, Mexico. She gained strength walking in the pool with a friend who had multiple sclerosis. Here, at the Puerto Fino Resort, Joan noticed women playing an ancient Chinese game called Mah Jongg. Joan recalled, "I was HOOKED." She is still playing, now in Wisconsin.

Joan returned to Puerto Vallarta each January-April with the exception of 2014. Now walking comfortably and with her employment days over, traveling was on the agenda again. Joan revisited much of Switzerland and Italy and well as visiting new countries/places. When landing in Venice "with way too much to haul around," she gave most away. Now, traveling with a small case on wheels with a backpack inside and a large purse, she was off to Budapest, Hungary, Warsaw and Krakow in Poland, Berlin and Hamburg in Germany and finally, visiting a friend in Prague, Czech Republic. "It was an adventure; Eastern Europe was rebuilding. I was tired, and headed home."

Back home in Wisconsin again, Joan cut her own wood with her chainsaw to use in the wood-burning stove throughout the long winter months. She spun yarn from Australian wool and knit various clothing articles. She sewed hats, shoes, slippers and clothing from tanned animal pelts.

When the warm days and cool nights of spring arrive, it was time for maple syrup tapping. First, drilling the tap hole, then inserting a spile (object to hang a bucket on) and immediately starting the flow of the sap. The sap must then be boiled down at a ratio of 40:1 (forty gallons makes one gallon of syrup)! It is definitely a "labor of love."

As the balmy days of summer approached, Joan loved to relax in her hammock permanently installed in her screen porch overlooking the beautiful wooded area. With a book in hand, she often dozed off listening to the birds, loons, and migrating water fowl sing their seasonal songs. She cultivated a vegetable garden and a flower garden, watched the bear, deer, foxes and birds enjoy her property as well. A mama bear with her two cubs meandered on to the property for lunch at her feeder. While Joan watched, mama stopped to nurse her two youngsters, then wandered back into the woods.

Give me a home where the deer and bear roam!

Friends from the Milwaukee area began to vacation in Puerto Vallarta. Joan soon joined them during the winter months. She took a yoga class, walked the beach daily picking up litter along the way, and "occasionally had the opportunity of rescuing a misdirected sea turtle."

In 2021, realizing most of her Puerto Vallarta friends were no longer able to spend winters there, Joan decided she would stay home for the winter. Here, she would use her snow blower to plow out her 150-foot hillside dirt driveway. She was comfortable living many miles from shops and facilities. Her caring cat, Barney, kept her company. Occasionally, her feline friend would share with her a half-eaten mouse—once deposited in her bed!

Joan continued to play Mah Jongg and often invited ladies to play on a Sunday afternoon. She loved to cook, so a wonderful lunch (with wine) was always included!

During the fall of 2022, Joan was clearing some brush on her property and was stung by a wasp--not once, but twice! By the second sting she knew she was in trouble and hurried inside to take Benadryl. Within moments she was lying on the bathroom floor, "feeling the life go out" of her body. Luckily, a good friend had just arrived and was able to call 911. An ambulance from nearby Presque Isle was dispatched. Joan was resuscitated and now carries an EpiPen when she is outdoors.

It wasn't the first time a serious health issue had affected her life. There was the broken back in 2010. Prior to that, in 1985 after a hiking trip in California with the Sierra Club, Joan developed weakness and exhaustion, difficulty when walking, and a foggy memory. She suffered symptoms for three years, finally went to Mayo Clinic where she was diagnosed with Lymes Disease. She was prescribed Penicillin then and, if and when, symptoms recurred.

The first verse of a poem written for me by my late husband, Bob Sandlin, when we moved to northern Wisconsin goes something like this:

There's a in this world where
I have found peace
Where the northern lights waver and glow.
Where the song of the loon
still rings on the water
And eagles cavort in the snow.
There's a place where the
sky and lakes define blue,
Where green is a color you breathe.
Where winter is white and autumn is fire
And love can take root and believe.

I'm sure Joan shared many of these feelings, but life was getting a bit difficult in the log home on the hill so she moved to a beautiful senior apartment in the village of Menomonee Falls, just north of Milwaukee.

She loves her apartment, but is confined more than she would like. A well-manicured lawn surrounding the buildings is sprayed regularly. Joan ended up in the hospital from a chemical reaction. She misses the Northwoods much more than she thought she would: the proximity of resources to walk on wooded trails, kayak on quiet rivers and swim in clear, unpolluted lakes gives way to traffic, cement, and crowded venues.

For an outdoors woman who finds "both challenge and growth through immersion in diverse circumstances," I would not be surprised if Joan would return to the Northwoods! In fact, we recently talked. Joan indicated she had wanted to spend a couple of months in Puerto Vallarta, but she could not find a rental for this winter.

She mentioned that she is looking for an apartment to rent—back in the Northwoods area she left. Whatever path Joan chooses will be a fulfilling journey through a life already full and exciting—but not over yet!

THE ORPHAN TRAIN
HAS LEFT THE STATION

During the last half of the nineteenth century close to 200,000 children were transported by train from eastern U.S. cities to mostly rural areas in the Midwest. Most of these youngsters were children of immigrants, often poor and destitute families. Some were orphaned, some abandoned, some homeless. Many ended up doing slave farm labor.

Charitable organizations, often supported by professionals and wealthy donors, were formed to help place the orphaned children into foster homes. Very few orphanages existed during this time period.

A minister, Charles Loring Brace, founded the Children's Aid Society in 1853, originally offering religious and vocational guidance. Later the organization offered shelters for runaways, lodging, education and assistance in finding jobs. But the numbers of the children in need was far greater than what the societies could handle. So, Brace came up with a new idea. He knew farms were in great need of labor and believed the farmers would welcome homeless children. The program seemed to work well in New York, Connecticut and Pennsylvania. Soon it was expanded to the Midwest.

The New York Foundling Home in New York City realized that they had become overloaded with young kids. One of these children was Marie Verzi, born in 1896. Few records were kept at that time; there were no adoption records.

Marie had a vague recollection "of sitting in a hallway and seeing a lady in the room across from me, feeding a child" at the local railroad station. Then someone carried Marie onto the train, helping her with her little red suitcase. A nurse usually accompanied the orphans to their destination and then returned to the East Coast city where she had originally boarded the train.

Marie was taken off the train at Felton, Minnesota, (2020 population: 177) bordering North Dakota. Here she lived with a lady, Mrs. Riel, who had two sons. One of the boys, George, was close to the same age as Marie. The two became playmates. Mrs. Riel called Marie "Mary," with emphasis on the "a." Two women with a last name of Goss lived downstairs from Mrs. Riel. Marie recalled that they made her a little red jacket and gave her a little wicker basket

Then, one day, and for some unknown reason, Father Maurice from a local Catholic church put Marie in a horse-drawn buggy and drove to a house owned by the Hoeflings. They lived north of Georgetown, near the Red River (later known as Koslosky Farm).

Marie recalled, "I don't know why, but I fought against going in. This was to be my new home." The family changed her name to Ophelia Hoefling.

The Hoeflings had a married daughter, Annie. There were two adopted sons: Jack, who was about thirteen years older than Ophelia, and Leo, just two years older than Ophelia. Leo would become Ophelia's new playmate.

Ophelia had an aunt and uncle who lived just north of the Hoefling home. They had three children. One of their children was staying at the Hoefling home while Ophelia's mother and aunt went into Georgetown. Ophelia described an incident that occurred while the women were away.

> There were large bags filled with straw, which served for mattresses. Leo managed to find a hole in the straw tick and pull out a large bunch of straw onto the floor. Then he lit a match and

started a fire on the floor. When he decided to put out the fire, which he was successful in doing, it had burned a big charred space—about two feet across. We got the broom and swept away the burnt straw that was left, but we couldn't seem to sweep away that big charred black space! It was needless to say what happened when Ma got home!

After losing their farm, the Hoeflings moved to another farm near Georgetown. As before, Ophelia walked to school during the cold Minnesota winters. Annie would rub snow on her frozen cheeks to take out the frost!

Country schools in the early 1900s consisted of grades one through eight in a small building, with one teacher who also had other duties such as starting a fire in the wood stove every morning before the children arrived. The teacher (Hulde Olin) offered Ophelia a job caring for her nephew and doing some housework. She tutored Ophelia in her lessons that included some high school subjects.

On August 29, 1909, Ophelia received her First Holy Communion. She had been taking instructions. Sometimes Father kept them a little longer and she was late getting to school. "People in Georgetown seemed to feel that church, work and school came in that order." Her teacher felt the order should be reversed!

Ophelia's First Communion.

In 1910 Miss Olin left to teach in Kent, Minnesota and asked Ophelia to come with her.

Instead, the next summer, Ophelia went to visit a housekeeper they had in Georgetown but who now lived in Fargo. She was offered a job as a telephone operator during their busy fall season for $30 per month. After that Ophelia worked for another telephone office in Moorhead, just

113

across the Red River from Fargo. She walked over the bridge to work, about 16 blocks. Here she was paid only $18 per month. She was soon asked to come back to Fargo as a position had opened up.

Ophelia (Age: 16)

When Ophelia found that could make twice what her hourly salary at the telephone company was, she enrolled in business school, graduating in 1915. To pay for school, she worked nights as a telephone switchboard operator. She slept on a cot next to the switchboard. When the buzzer rang, she would quickly wake up, take the call, and then lie down again. Ophelia remembered, "being young, it was easy to go back to sleep again!"

During her work at the telephone company, she had days off, so took a job for room and board, taking care of a little girl while her mom worked. Now, with a little extra money, she bought a piano on installment. Free lessons were offered with the purchase.

Ophelia enrolled in Fargo Central High School two weeks after school had resumed. Working nights, taking piano lessons, besides trying to study was just too much.

Ophelia resumed work, this time in the office of the phone company. She decided to attend night classes at Aaker's Business College to study stenography. Stenographers were getting paid twice what she was making now! Ophelia graduated the spring of 1915.

At school she met a gal with like interests and a like name: Othelia! Othelia and Ophelia would become lifelong friends.

Ophelia's first job after business school was a temporary one with J. D. Grant Accessory Company in Fargo. They sold car accessories that owners could apply to their cars. Then one day, Mr. Aaker from the business school called to say that a steady job in Hillsboro (North Dakota) National Bank was available. Ophelia got the job, but it was not what she wanted. Three months later she moved back for Fargo where she took a temporary job at the Globe-Gazette Printing Company doing bookkeeping and stenographic work

During this period of time, Ophelia's health deteriorated. Her doctor told her to get a good rest, so she resigned and spent the winter with Mrs. White, her former landlady in Fargo, who now lived in a sod house near Weldon, Montana (about 450 miles west of Fargo). Two of Ophelia's uncles, and their families, lived nearby.

Ophelia with friend Mary Spillum

It was the day before Thanksgiving when Ophelia got off the train. Mrs. White and her neighbor, Gouldie Erwin, arrived with a team of horses pulling a wagon. It was a full day's drive (about 45 miles) to their destination and darkness was setting in. There were deep cutbanks near the river's bends and Gouldie was taking several nips from a bottle. It was a scary trip, but they reached Weldon safely.

The day after Thanksgiving Gouldie asked Ophelia to go to a dance with her. She accepted, and though very tired, "danced every dance until morning!"

In February 1917 Ophelia left Weldon to attend her cousin's wedding in Vida, Montana. She stayed with her cousin's parents until spring, then returned to Weldon.

Local people convinced Ophelia to apply for a homestead in Montana. The state, in order to build up their population, was offering 160 acres free if the owner would stay five years. People flooded to Montana to apply.

In spring 1917 Ophelia returned to Fargo where she stayed with friends and worked for Remington Typewriter Company doing public stenographic work. In the fall she received word that her application for homestead filing had been accepted. So, she returned to Weldon.

Now she needed to find a job. So, she hitched a ride in the sled of a mail carrier going from Weldon to Oswego (a trip of close to 90 miles). It was snowing, and visibility was poor. They found a pair of sled tracks, not knowing where they led, and followed them as darkness set in. They finally heard a dog barking; that led them to see a light in a home where the family offered them supper and a stay overnight. Ophelia and the woman stayed in the small house; the two men slept in the barn!

By the next morning the snow had stopped falling and they went on to Oswego. From here Ophelia took a train to Wolf Point, about 12 miles away, but couldn't find work there. Then she learned that the Fort Peck Indian Agency near Wolf Point was looking for a stenographer. She applied—and was hired!

The superintendent of the agency offered Ophelia a room at his family home. She, and other employees, ate meals at the Agency Mess Hall. Winter snows were so deep that fences were covered; somehow Ophelia was able to climb over them to get to work!

The Land Office in Washington insisted that Ophelia return to the homestead. She left the Agency in May 1918 with a horse and buggy she had purchased. Her trip took her to Wolf Point and Oswego. Leaving Oswego, she drove onto a ferry crossing the Missouri River. It was still light out, so she decided to drive on. But darkness came suddenly and she could no longer see the road. She unhitched her horse and tied her to the buggy, where the two slept until sunrise. She then drove on to Weldon.

Ophelia and her horse

One summer, Ophelia decided to visit old friends, the Wambachs, so she put some clothes in a pillow case, placed it on the back of her saddle and rode horseback 45 miles (usually a two-day trip).

Ophelia visited the same friends another summer, now with a buggy. "As I look back, I can't figure out how I found the way as there were no roads across that part of the country; and, of course, there were no such things as road signs!" She knew what direction she wanted to go, and "just cut across the hills!"

One day Ophelia's horse was startled and threw her off. She landed hard on her right shoulder and was taken to the nearest doctor—25 miles away! The shoulder was cracked, so it was taped and for the next five weeks she wore a sling. The horse that bucked her off her saddle was long gone. When finally found, the horse was with her little colt!

At Weldon, Ophelia yearned to dance, but could only watch because of her shoulder. A young man named Phillip Gleason, an immigrant from Ireland, sat out many of the dances with her. She had met him before when she lived at Mrs. White's home, but this time he was paying a lot of attention to her!

A note of interest: Phil could never become a U.S. citizen because he had a "criminal" record. He was jailed for one night for delivering booze for his boot-legging brother-in-law, Jack!

Phil invited Ophelia to a July 4th celebration. At the party he invited her to go for a walk in the nearby woods. He paused on the path, then said, "Now I want you to take me seriously and not laugh at me." He went on to say, "I would like to kidnap you. I love you. Don't give me your answer now, but think about it." Surprised, Ophelia did not give him an immediate answer, but did promise him she would think about it!

Ophelia went back to Fargo/Morehead for the winter. It was not until she returned to Weldon in the spring of 1919 that she accepted Phil's proposal. First, she decided to cook for some sheepherders out in the hills. She slept in a covered wagon; the men slept in the second wagon. After two weeks of working for the men there, she "had enough of the lonely life." Phil had come out to see her and she went back to Weldon with him.

Prior to their wedding, Ophelia worked at the Court House in Circle, Montana, then went back to Fargo where she worked for the Fargo Forum, the major newspaper in Fargo. She took a couple of months off, after problems with her eyes, then returned to Weldon to "prove up and get title to my homestead."

Then, it was back to her job at the Fargo newspaper. Phil joined her at the end of October, and they were married November 6, 1922. They honeymooned in Minneapolis. The couple lived on the homestead land for five years--farming six months each year. Ironically, it was later discovered that this homestead land was on the Williston Oil Basis. Had she remained a homesteader, Ophelia would probably have become a rich woman!

After the Gleasons started a family, Ophelia left the homestead land as there were no Catholic churches in the vicinity. She wanted her children to grow up Catholic, (DNA results, revealed years later, indicated that her mother was Jewish!)

Phil was hired by the Polka Dot Cereal Company in Fargo. They rented the upstairs of Ophelia's brother's house. Eventually, the family moved out. Phil and Ophelia bought the house and rented out the downstairs.

Ophelia left her job at the Forum a few months before baby Ellen was born on January 14, 1924. That March, Ophelia's dad passed away.

Upkeep on the Moorhead home was getting too much for Ma. So, a neighbor removed a large room, attached to a smaller room, from their house. The larger room was moved to the back of the Gleason's home. "Ma rented out her big home and moved into the backyard!"

During the summer of 1925, Phil's company could no longer pay his salary so gave him an old Ford Coup, the family's first car! On a trip to Weldon to try to sell the homestead, the couple stopped at a Ford agency. Phil surprised Ophelia. "Come and see our new car." It was another coup. They were expecting their second child, so Ophelia made Phil trade it back for a four-door sedan!

Sister Ellen was now two years old. Second girl, Kathryn, was born January 29, 1926.

Ellen and Kathryn, a couple years later.

In 1928 Phil was transferred to Council Bluffs, Iowa, where he continued to work as a salesman—but now for the Dwarfies Cereal Company, an offshoot from Polka Dot.

Daughter Patricia was born on February 6, 1930. The family soon moved to a cottage on Lake Manawa near Omaha, Nebraska. When a larger house was available, they moved again— nearby, still on the Lake.

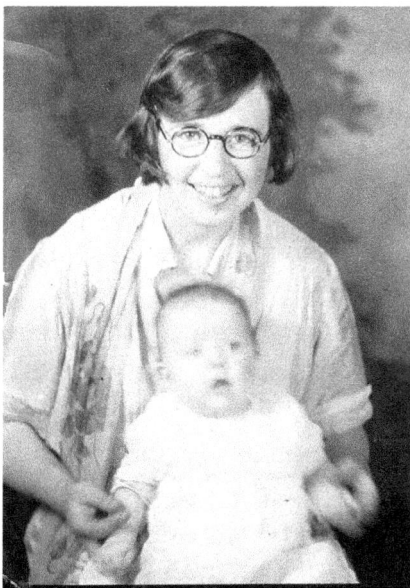

Proud Mom!

In autumn 1931 the Gleasons rented an apartment in Council Bluffs, Iowa. They kept the house in Lake Manawa to have easy access to the hospital where daughter Phyllis was born on December 12. When weather became warmer, they returned to the Lake.

Patricia was diagnosed with diphtheria about the 22nd of February and died in the hospital on February 29, 1932. Shortly after the funeral Phil was laid off and went to work for a company selling Blue Barrel laundry soap. It was a sad year.

By fall 1933 Phil was offered a job in Minneapolis working for the Georgie Porgie Cereal Company, advertising the cereal and singing Irish songs on a local radio station.

Note: The company was named after an 1841 ballad that went something like this:

> Georgie Porgie, pudding and pie,
> Kissed the girls and made them cry,
> When the girls came out to play,
> Georgie Porgie ran away.

Across the road from the radio station was a little plaque shop. Ophelia began taking lessons in plaque painting and soon began teaching the skill in their home.

Ophelia, licking the pudding spoon!

Phil resigned from Georgie Porgie after missing a salary check one week and started a theatre circuit with an acquaintance. After two months and poor financial gains, they moved to New Ulm and opened a theatre there. After another couple of months, that endeavor folded too.

In the meantime, Ophelia had started a plaque painting class. They now were living with the couple involved in the theatre failures. The men tried once again, opening a theatre in Winthrop. Business here was good, but income not good enough to support two families in the small town.

So, Phil and Ophelia bought a plaque shop in Minneapolis in spring of 1935. Ophelia worked in the shop, living in the back part of the shop. Phil got a job with Sim's Breakfast Food Company, working mostly in the La Crosse, Wisconsin area. He was soon laid off.

Ophelia had a girl working for her in Minneapolis and decided to lease a dress shop in La Crosse, Wisconsin to be nearer to her husband. It was not disclosed when she signed the lease, but the rent was to be raised the very next month. A few months later Ophelia was able to get her money back and leave the business.

Phil, now laying linoleum, learned to make the white plaques himself. They rented a duplex just a few blocks from the shop where he made the plaques. By 1937 the family was selling their plaques, calling on retail stores from Wisconsin to North Dakota. The older girls, Ellen (age 13) and Kathryn (age 11), took care of the shop while their parents traveled.

In the fall of 1938 Ophelia became pregnant again. They bought an old, large house that they could receive an income from renting out rooms. The house came complete with tenants!

The bank had refused to give out a mortgage loan until the outside of the house was painted. According to Ophelia, "the outside of the house looked terrible; it hadn't been painted for years." But, instead of painting, they put on asbestos shingles. The house had a small dirt basement. Phil enlarged it, put in workbenches and began making plaques there.

The Gleasons last child and only boy, David, was born on April 23, 1939. That fall Phil drove to Moorhead "and brought Ma home with him to spend the winter with us." She left in spring, anxious to start her garden. Ma suffered a stroke and passed away in January 1941.

By spring of 1948, shops were selling plaques that were spray-painted; there was no longer a demand for the hand-painted ones. Phil could not find work, so Ophelia got a job at a Gamble-Skogmo warehouse that June.

Phil developed colon cancer in 1951 and had surgery. Ophelia felt she needed to bring in more money. She passed a Civil Service examination and took a job with the U.S. Navy Audit Office in 1952. She retired in 1961 and did temporary office work at different places.

Ophelia at work in the Navy Audit Office

Ophelia never learned to drive. Phil had been a salesman for many years, traveling with their only car. Now was the time: Ophelia got her driver's license at age 69!

Phil passed away on January 10, 1967 after many operations caused by his cancer. Ophelia moved into the upstairs apartment owned by grandson Bruce (Ellen's boy). Later she rented a Senior Housing apartment in Minneapolis. Her last move was to a Senior Housing apartment in Long Lake, Minnesota—closer to Kathryn and her family.

Ophelia passed away on May 13, 1988—just two hours before her 93rd birthday.

Ophelia Gleason was a smart and talented woman who always provided for herself. She was the main breadwinner while raising five children.

In Shakespeare's "Hamlet," Ophelia was in love with Hamlet. She represented beauty and selflessness. In fact, the name "Ophelia" means "Help" or "Advantage." The Hebrew definition is "a bitter sea to the demons"; Catholic version is "guide to the sea...lady, teacher." She was all of those things...and more.

Ophelia Marie Hoefling Gleason was a resourceful pioneer woman, working outside the home, traveling by horseback—or whatever means she could—to many and varied jobs. She always tried to improve herself and her situation by furthering her education and taking on better jobs to earn more money to support her family. She was a female homesteader, did all the family financial business, and experienced many hardships. Grass never grew under her feet! Life was not easy, but she persevered.

Much of the above story was passed on by Ophelia herself, through journals she passed down to family members. Her daughter, Kathryn Dumas of Long Lake, Minnesota and granddaughter, Marilyn Gabert of Boulder Junction, Wisconsin, shared pictures and more information for this story. I believe that they inherited many of Ophelia's traits

PEACE IN THE VALLEY

There was a song, Peace in the Valley (For Me) written by Thomas A. Dorsey while he traveled by train through southern Indiana. Dorsey was a Christian evangelist born in 1899 who was influential in the development of early gospel music.

World War II began in September of 1939 and tensions were mounting. Dorsey wondered why. Gazing out the train window he observed cows, horses and sheep grazing together. He wondered why we all couldn't live in peace like the animals of different species that he observed.

There will be peace in the valley
Oh Lord I pray
There will be peace in the valley for me,
There'll be no sadness, no sorrow
No trouble, trouble I see
There will be peace in the valley for me,
some day.

The song, sung by Elvis Presley on the Ed Sullivan show in 1957, became a hit. Elvis crooned; and as a teenager, I swooned!

I met Pat Condon when I joined the Sly Fox Ski Club in Appleton, Wisconsin--the largest city in

133

the Fox River Valley (commonly known as "the Valley.") Here Pat taught learning-disabled students, grade one through six, for 20 years.

Skiing was just one "peace" of Pat's life!

During the 1960s Pat became involved with Beyond War, an organization espousing the Domino Theory: That if one country falls to the enemy, more countries would fall also--like a line of dominoes. She was opposed to the Vietnam War and activities that led to wars in countries like Iraq, Afghanistan and Pakistan.

On the countertop in Pat's kitchen lies a large paper banner reading "War is Not the Answer" put out by the Quaker Friends Committee on USSR National Legislation. Pat supports societies such as the Quaker-based American Friends Service Committee that work for peace and social justice in the United States and around the world. She is a member of Unitarian Universalist Association advocating their work towards human rights and justice.

Pat was involved with three Peace Concerts during the mid-1980s to help fund Sister City International, a program that promotes citizen diplomacy, international exchange and building bridges of understanding across borders.

The first concert was held at the Lawrence University Concert Auditorium in Appleton, Wisconsin. Over 700 people listened to a local folk group, Crystal River Trio. (Note: My late husband, Bob Sandlin, was a member of this talented trio. The following year Crystal River "opened" for the Kingston Trio at the Peace Concert, opting not to sing any of the songs that the Trio had written and/or recorded! After the concert we all socialized at the Paper Valley Hotel.)

Pat studied the Russian language for two years in preparation for a scheduled trip to Pyatigorsk, Appleton's designated city in the Sister Cities program.

Pat relates, "the highlight of the trip was the eventual continued exchanges of Russian students studying in the U.S. and development of a wood business in Russia."

Later, Appleton would pair with Kurgan in north central USSR. Out of this convention, Pat explains, "came the formation of Physicians for Social Responsibility, which continued their medical services with needy Russians."

In 1990 Pat taught students in grades five and six in Tuam, Ireland. An art project developed for the students involved making paper sails with peace symbols and messages on them. Pat took the students' art works back to Appleton. She explains, "There is a tradition of floating little handmade sailboats on the Fox River in memory/retribution of the U.S. bombing Japan." She adds, "We had a picture and article in the Appleton Post Crescent.

Another trip with a study group involving interconnectedness of the United States with Central America and Mexico took Pat to Cuernavaca, Mexico. Here, at the Cuernavaca Center for Intercultural Dialog on Development, Pat was involved with Bible study and assessing poverty as well as visiting Mexican wonders and attending Cathedral and Ballet Folklorico. She noted, "A highlight of the trip was the establishment of a Mexican Women's

Cooperative to create work in common for the women and a safe play place for children."

Pat retired from teaching in 1994 and moved to Apache Junction, Arizona. Now, twice divorced, she reverted to her maiden name, Flahart. (Flahart, it is believed, was derived from O'Flaharty—a common surname of families who resided in the northern part of Ireland.)

Here, near Phoenix and just below the Superstition Mountains, Pat continued her peace endeavors by "writing letters for Amnesty International, helping with Peace Concerts involving weekly Sunday meetings with ASU students, and giving donations." She adds, "I sign email and my cards "Peace, Pat.""

While living in Apache Junction, Pat volunteered for twelve years at an elementary school and also at the Learning Center at the local library in a preschool program where she tutored an eighth-grade student and a 74-year-old man from Wisconsin!

Peace endeavors continued when Pat became a member of the Unitarian Church in Chandler, Arizona. Here she attended a Buddhism study group that led her to sponsor Peace concerts in Tempe, Arizona. Political science students from Arizona State University joined Pat and her Unitarian friends in planning concerts featuring local musicians and bands (as she had done in Appleton, Wisconsin). Their group sponsored three concerts in three years.

Peace is described as "freedom from war, public disorder, disagreement and peace of mind."

Pat nurtured her own peace of mind and body by dancing! As an eighth grader, her mother taught her to do the Charleston. This would come in handy later, when as a freshman at Loretto Heights College in Denver, Colorado she danced the Charleston in a special college show. Pat took ballet lessons during her high school years in Rapid City, South Dakota. She paid for them with money earned from babysitting and work at the local Chuck Wagon restaurant., She also danced in "Carousel" and "Show Boat", the latter in Neenah Wisconsin, with the Riverside Players.

Pat enjoyed Friday night dances at her Cathedral High School. Her main dance partner was Dick (a School of Mines college freshman). He loved to jitterbug—especially to the song "Rock Around the Clock" (recorded by Bill Haley and the Comets). Pat recalls "one of the priests would engage the boys in conversation while the girls sat on chairs waiting to be asked to dance." (I'm not sure if there was a motive to that, but I remember that our principal monitored dances at my high school. A dance called the "Dirty Bop" was outlawed. That dance today would be "milk-toast" mild!)

Dance classes started in Appleton, Wisconsin. Pat's first husband danced very little. A couple of decades later Pat attended Line Dance classes and admits "she spent a lot of money on Fred Astaire dance lessons" as well.

Pat continued dance classes in Apache Junction, taking both tap and ballet lessons to prepare for an advertised dance program. She also helped with makeup and with preschool-age children.

Through dancers in the Unity Church, Pat joined a folkdance group who visited retirement communities and assisted living homes. She was the "new kid on the block" joining men and women who had been folk dancing for many years.

Next it was clog dancing and, finally, Zumba and line dance classes that occurred just six blocks from her home in Ahwatukee. Pat loves to line dance because "women don't need a male partner." One song they dance to is "I Love My Life." Pat feels the significance of the title as she "LOVES how dance has been an important part of my life." Pat is very close to her son, two daughters and grandchildren—none of whom followed in her dancing footsteps!

Pat's ancestors lived in Protestant sectors of Ireland. One of my favorite Irish songs that Crystal River Trio often sang is "Star of the County Down," which was written by Cathal McGarvey in 1910. It reminds me of Pat, with her Irish good looks, clogging to the music of her ancestors! The first verse follows:

Near to Banbridge Town,
There In the County Down
One morning last July,
Down a boreen green
Came a sweet colleen,
And she smiled as she passed me by;
Well, she looked so sweet
From her two bare feet
To the sheen of her nut-brown hair.
Such a coaxing elf,
Sure I shook myself
To make sure I was truly there.

Pat has a son and two daughters. One of her girls is named Colleen!

Dancing brought Pat peace of mind. She relates, "My thinking is that peace starts first in me, radiates out to my family, and then to the universe." People have sought peace throughout eternity. Pat's view echoes a quote by Lao Tzu (570-490 BC):

If there is to be peace in the world, There must be peace in the nations.

If there is to be peace in the nations, There must be peace in the cities.

If there is to be peace in the cities, There must be peace between neighbors.

If there is to be peace in the home, There must be peace in the heart.

MAY PEACE BE WITH YOU!